AQA

GCSE ENGLISH
Teacher's Book

Rachel Redford

AQA ENGLISH/SPECIFICATION B

OXFORD
UNIVERSITY PRESS

OXFORD
UNIVERSITY PRESS

Great Clarendon Street, Oxford OX2 6DP

Oxford University Press is a department of the University of Oxford.
It furthers the University's objective of excellence in research,
scholarship, and education by publishing worldwide in

Oxford New York

Auckland Bangkok Buenos Aires Cape Town Chennai
Dar es Salaam Delhi Hong Kong Istanbul Karachi Kolkata
Kuala Lumpur Madrid Melbourne Mexico City Mumbai Nairobi
São Paulo Shanghai Taipei Tokyo Toronto

Oxford is a registered trade mark of Oxford University Press
in the UK and in certain other countries

British Library Cataloguing in Publication Data

Data available

ISBN 0 19 831497 3

10 9 8 7 6 5 4 3 2 1

Printed in Great Britain by Alden Press Ltd, Oxford

Acknowledgements

The Publisher would like to thank the following for permission to
reproduce photographs:

Corel Professional Photos: p 49, 50, 57, 84; The Portable Antiquities
Scheme (Kent) www.finds.org.uk p 87

Cover photographs by Alamy (background); Corel Professional Photos:
bottom; PA Photos: top (Ken Saro-Wiwa); Photodisc: second from top;
The Portable Antiquities Scheme (Kent) www.finds.org.uk: third from
top (Bronze Age gold cup).

We are grateful for permission to include the following copyright
material in this book:

John Agard: 'Rainbow' from *Mangoes and Bullets: Selected and New Poems
1972-1984* (Pluto Press, 1985), reproduced by permission of the author,
c/o Caroline Sheldon Literary Agency.
E. A. Brininstool: 'The Last Drive', published in *Cowboy Poetry* edited
by Julie Saffel (Castle Books, 2001).
Caroline Davies: extract from 'She was simply the most magical
grandmother', *The Daily Telegraph*, 2.4.02, copyright © Telegraph Group
Ltd 2002, reproduced by permission of the Telegraph Group Ltd.
Exodus: extract from 'Multi Activity' brochure 2002-3, reproduced by
permission of Exodus Travels Ltd.
Fauna: extract from 'Chicken Meat Production' leaflet, reproduced by
permission of The Friends of Animals Under Abuse, P O Box 156,
Cardiff, CF5 5YD.
Carlo Gébler: extract from *Father and I: A Memoir* (Little Brown & Co,
2000), reproduced by permission of Antony Harwood Ltd.
Petrus Augustus de Genestat: 'Such is Holland' translated by
Adriaan Barnouw from *Coming After: An Anthology of Poetry from the Low
Countries* (1948), copyright © 1948 by The Trustees of Rutgers College
in New Jersey, reproduced by permission of Rutgers University Press.
Michael Gove: extract from 'The cloud inside my head' and 'Flying:
The facts' by David Mattin, *The Times*, 8.5.02, copyright © Times
Newspapers Ltd, London, 2002, reproduced by permission of News
International plc.
Roy Hattersley: extract from 'Vindicated!', *Evening Standard*, 5.2.02,
reproduced by permission of Lord Hattersley.
Christopher Hitchens: extract from 'Comment and Analysis', *The
Guardian*, 1.4.02, copyright © Christopher Hitchens 2002, reproduced
by permission of Guardian Newspapers Ltd.
Mark Honingsbaum: extract from article on Venezuela, *High Life*,
September 2000, reproduced by permission of the author and Cedar
Communications.
Nick Hornby: extract from 'I'm Like a Bird' in 'Music', *Granta* 76,
Winter 2001, reproduced by permission of PFD on behalf of the Nick
Hornby.
Frederico García Lorca: 'Canción de jinete', © copyright Herederos
de Frederico García Lorca, translated by Alan S. Trueblood as 'Rider's
Song', copyright © Herederos de Frederico García Lorca and Alan S.
Trueblood. All rights reserved. For information regarding rights and
permissions, please contact lorca@artslaw.co.uk or William Peter
Kosmas, Esq., 8 Franklin Square, London W14 9UU. This poem can be
found in *Frederico García Lorca Selected Poems* (Penguin Books Ltd,
London, 2001).
Ian McDonald: 'Georgetown Children' from *Jaffo the Calypsonian*
(Peepal Tree, 1994), reproduced by permission of the publisher.
Jenny Madden: headline and captions for 'Web of Deceit', *The
Guardian* 'Women', 22.4.02, copyright © Jenny Madden 2002, repro-
duced by permission of Guardian Newspapers Ltd.
Ken Saro-Wiwa: 'The True Prison' published in *Captured Voices* edited
by Janna Letts and Fiona Whytehead (Victor Gollancz, 1999).
Francis Spufford: extract from *The Child That Books Built* (Faber &
Faber Ltd, 2000), reprinted by permission of the publishers.
Vaidehi (Janaki Srinivasamurthy): 'Girl in the Kitchen', translated
from Kannada by A. K. Ramanujan from *In Their Own Voice: Penguin
Anthology of Contemporary Indian Poets* edited by Arlene R. K. Zide
(Penguin Books, India, 1993), reprinted by permission of Dr A. R. K.
Zide.

It has not been possible to trace and contact all copyright holders of
material included before publication. If notified the publisher under-
takes to rectify any errors or omissions at the earliest opportunity.

CONTENTS

These 96 pages are full of all kinds of invaluable support and resources:

◆ The book is for *all* teachers in *all* kinds of learning institutions. Newly qualified teachers and those who feel isolated in colleges and special schools will find it particularly invaluable.

◆ It has been designed for use in tandem with the accompanying *English Students' Book,* which offers thorough teaching and practice to build all the skills needed for the examinations, presented in comprehensive step-by-step units.

◆ The texts have been carefully selected to capture the interest of all students, not just those in school, but also the mix of students in further education from 16-year-old re-take students to the fully mature. This makes the *Teacher's Book,* like the *Students' Book,* an excellent resource for distance learners and all those studying at home, as well as at school and college.

◆ The texts are brief and the tasks set are not complete essays, but focused exercises. This is to give students a sense of achievement and to encourage precision in their writing.

◆ All the assessment objectives of the 2004 specifications for Reading and Writing in English examinations have been incorporated into the guidance and tasks given to students. They have been presented in clear, student-friendly language.

The book is in three parts:

1 POETRY FROM DIFFERENT CULTURES

This is the new element in the examination from 2004, and it is fully explained here for teachers. Detailed information and guidance is given on: the kinds of poems which will be selected; areas for focus in teaching the pre-released booklet; and the technical terms students will need for analysing poetry.

The assessment objectives are set out and clearly explained, with full illustration of the kinds of points students at different levels will make to achieve them. Hints, guidance, and illustration are focused throughout on the full range of student ability.

Two complete examination-style poetry questions are included, one for Foundation Tier and one for Higher Tier. The answers are worked through in detail with full examples and illustration. The four poems referred to in the questions are supplied.

Four additional poems are given – two suggested for Foundation Tier study, and two for Higher Tier. Each is introduced by a contextualizing paragraph, and they are 'brainstormed' with suggestions for analysis and interpretation. In addition, these four poems are provided on photocopy masters (PCMs).

2 SUPPORT FOR LESS ABLE STUDENTS

'Less able' in this context means those students who are just below, and well below, Grade C. They will probably make basic errors in their writing in the examination, and their reading and interpretation skills are limited. All the step-by-step guidance given for students to work through in the reading and writing sections is carefully designed and structured to improve these students' skills.

The guidance units are designed to be absolutely clear, friendly, and stimulating for students working on their own or with minimal teacher help. The Reading to Write units are specially designed for students to practise basic skills entirely without teacher help. These are fully photocopiable.

The Writing units include PCMs to help with planning and organization. Full details of the skills covered in the different units are given in the introduction to the Support for Less Able Students, on pages 32–3.

3 EXTENSION FOR MORE ABLE STUDENTS

'More able' students are students who are expected to achieve Grade B or higher. They are competent writers with a good level of accuracy, and they read with understanding and interpretation.

Able students are sometimes not given the stimulation and help which could lift their skills – and their grades. This section is designed to fill that gap. The purpose of the guidance and tasks given here is to extend their capabilities so that they can read and write showing high-order Grade A and A* skills.

The varied texts have been selected to challenge, provoke, and stimulate students and to elicit advanced reading and writing skills. Students can work through the units on their own, or with minimal teacher help.

The Writing units offer detailed guidance on extending students' skills and include PCMs. The Reading to Write unit is specially designed for students to practise higher order skills entirely without teacher help, and is fully photocopiable.

Full details are given in the introduction to the Extension for More Able Students section, on pages 74–5.

Poetry from different cultures

Poetry from different cultures is the new element in the examination from 2004. The pre-released booklet, which will be distributed each January, will present all the poems required for study. There will be eight to ten poems in the booklet which will represent varying degrees of challenge, but which will not be coded 'Foundation' or 'Higher'.

In the examination, the Foundation and Higher tiers will each have a different unseen poem, and the question will direct candidates to a different poem in the booklet with which to compare the unseen poem. Students, of course, will not know beforehand which poem will be named. Different poems will be named in the Foundation tier and the Higher tier, and in the summer and autumn examinations.

For practice study before the exam, the AQA specimen papers include a selection of poems, the AQA support booklet provides more, the OUP *Students' Book* more again, and this *Teacher's Book* includes yet more! The poems come from all over the globe: from ancient Greece and Japan, to wild west cowboys and contemporary India and the Caribbean.

Clearly, these poems come from very different places and cultures. Those presented in the OUP *Students' Book* and here in the *Teacher's Book* range from Ken Saro-Wiwa's powerful poem on 'The True Prison' written before his execution in Nigeria in 1995, to Lorca's account of a mysterious horseman riding a black pony beneath a full red moon, and to John Agard's jaunty celebration of a rainbow. Whatever the poems are about, the culture from which they come will be different from Britain's – although with our cultural mix, it is perhaps impossible to define 'British culture'. All these poems have been carefully chosen to present an interesting spread of contemporary and historical cultures, and of geographical settings – as well as for their appeal to mature students and school pupils. The two love poems, 'just in case' by Jean 'Binta' Breeze and Hitomaro's 'On Going from the Province of Iwami' (*Students' Book* page 62), and Ken Saro-Wiwa's 'The True Prison', were chosen with mature students particularly in mind. But the most important reason of all is that studying them will be enjoyable and worthwhile.

Teachers do not need to feel concerned that they are being asked to teach an area of poetry which is entirely new to them. They will not be expected to provide the **background** to these poems. In the pre-released booklet, and in the 'brainstormed' poems in this book, there is a brief paragraph which puts each poem succinctly in its context. For example, in the AQA specimen pre-released booklet, there are two poems about peasant women by the Polish poet Anna Swir. The paragraph introducing the poem includes the information that she lived at the time of the communist régime in Poland, and that she used to accompany her artist father on his painting expeditions into the countryside. This helps to throw light on her two poems about peasant women. Dates, political or social background to the countries, distinctive features of culture, landscape or language, and biographical detail are other kinds of information which are included as relevant. Culturally specific references which might be obscure are glossed.

On the examination paper for both tiers, this sentence appears after the question:

Candidates are reminded to comment on the cultural aspects of the poems.

This should not worry students or teachers. The poems have been carefully chosen to take account of this directive. For example, an Ecuadorian poet has written a poem about the flight of a hummingbird. It is a delicate poem, but what she says about nature and love could equally well have been said by a British poet writing about a kingfisher. Although the Ecuadorian poem *is* 'poetry from different cultures', it is not one which would be chosen for examination study. The poems selected for study are those in which the different cultural perspectives of the poets, and the different aspects of their countries, customs, and language, will be expressed in some way – whether it be the '*bronco's tireless, steady pace*' in the cowboy's dreams in 'The Last Drive', or the elements in society which Saro-Wiwa believes have turned '*our free world into a dreary prison*'.

The 'different culture-ness' is, therefore, an **integral part** of each poem, and will be studied as the students analyse the poem. It will not be something separate which teachers will be expected to teach. When students answer the structured examination questions, they will be commenting on the **cultural aspects** of the poems. The directive on the examination paper need not, therefore, worry either students or teachers.

Translations

Inevitably, a number of these poems will have been translated – a fascinating topic in itself, but not one which teachers need be concerned about. Ezra Pound took considerable translator's licence when he 'translated' poems such as 'The River Merchant's Wife: A Letter' from the eighth century Chinese poet, Li Po (AQA specimen pre-released booklet). He even used the Japanese form of Li Po's name, Rihaku, because he was working from Japanese translations of the Chinese! Other translators, however, like A. K. Ramanujan who has translated from the Indian language, Kannada, in 'Girl in the Kitchen' in this book, have taken great pains to represent the original faithfully. The translator's name will be given, and if the translation is of particular interest or significance, it will be mentioned in the contextualization. The poems, however, will be studied as they are on the page: students do not need to know anything about the translation and they will not be tested on any aspect of it.

Teaching the pre-released booklet

In the past, pre-released texts have been definitively 'taught' and students have relied heavily on their annotated booklets in the examination, usually to their disadvantage. They have frequently copied out chunks of annotation without making it answer the question, or they have been so anxious to write down all their annotation, that they have given scant attention to the unseen text. Their comments on the unseen texts have shown that, in fact, students' responses are more relevant and fresh when they are not relying on annotated, pre-taught texts.

The role of the pre-released poems will be different from previously pre-released texts now that:

◆ beginning with the examination in 2005, pre-released booklets must not be annotated

◆ the focus of the questions in the examination will be on the unseen poem.

The poems in the pre-released booklet are not 'set texts' as for the English Literature examination. They are practice springboards for teasing out meaning and interpretations and analysing language effects, so that students will know how to approach the unseen poem in the examination. It would be sensible for the approach to the pre-released poems in the classroom to be the same as that advised for the student in the examination when faced with an unseen poem. Students can then replicate their classroom strategy in the examination.

PRE-RELEASED AND UNSEEN POEMS: AREAS FOR FOCUS

Reading the pre-released poems

These are the Assessment Objectives for Reading relevant to poetry from different cultures:

> Candidates are required to demonstrate the ability to:
>
> 2.1 read, with insight and engagement, making appropriate references to texts and developing and sustaining interpretations of them;
>
> 2.4 select material appropriate to purpose, collate material from different sources, and make cross references;
>
> 2.5 understand and evaluate how writers use linguistic, structural, and presentational devices to achieve their effects, and comment on the ways language varies and changes.

Understanding, interpretation, and insight

These skills are hierarchical, although they obviously overlap. Taking 'Rainbow' as an example, students who appreciate that the poet is expressing an enthusiastic response to a rainbow have *understood* what the poem is about. Those who refer to particular lines and comment on the poet's admiration for the creator of the rainbow are *interpreting*; whilst those who quote phrases to illustrate the poet's slightly outrageous humour are reading with *insight*. Giving students practice in selecting brief quotation to illustrate the main points **economically** would be very useful for them.

Making cross references

Students will be asked to make some kind of comparison between an unseen and a pre-released poem in the examination, so practice in making *cross references* is definitely useful. Comparisons, of course, involve finding similarities as well as differences, and could be focused on any aspect from theme and mood to language or cultural elements. Students could, for example, explore the different ways in which the rainbow is presented in 'Rainbow', and rain and wet is presented in 'Such is Holland!'; how the theme of longing is presented in 'Girl in the Kitchen' and 'Mal du Pays'; or, for the more able, how the lessons learned through adversity, and the tone, compare in 'A Blindman Sings' and 'The True Prison'.

Analysis of language and verse structure

When students study prose passages, they are used to analysing sentence structure as part of language analysis. In poetry analysis, they will be expected to demonstrate that same skill, which will be part of understanding and appreciating the verse structure. Language analysis of poetry includes comment on words and phrases, but the **discriminating skill** will be to analyse the **effect** of the features selected, not merely to give a description of them, or identify them. For example in 'The Last Drive', the aged cowboy's vision of the *'broad-hatted men, bronzed, fearless, bold'* could be **selected** because it is a vivid description of the strong cowboys he remembers. To analyse the **effect** of the line, the student would need to comment on the way the multiple adjectives with their connotations of masculinity, strength, and courage add power and visual impact to the description of the cowboys. The most able would explain how this idealized image is appropriate to the old man's rose-tinted imagination, and to the romanticized, cliché-ed tone of the whole poem.

Technical terms for poetry

This is the first time that students will have to write about poetry in their English examination. How many technical terms do students need to know, in addition to those they are already familiar with through their analysis of prose? A poet chooses to construct a poem in a way which suits his or her purpose: whether it resembles prose, cut up apparently randomly into lines (see 'just in case', *Students' Book*, page 62), or whether it is in structured, rhyming quatrains (see 'Once in a Lifetime, Snow', *Students' Book* page 69), the structure is an integral part of the poem.

Although the main focus of the questions in the examination will not be on the rhythm, rhyme scheme or verse structure of the poems, it would be helpful for students to have some knowledge of technical terms so that they can describe or analyse those features where relevant. What follows is a guide, not a definitive list.

Basic terms

Verse/stanza	to be able to say a poem is written in stanzas/verses
Rhythm	to recognize that there is or is not a rhythmic pattern
Rhyme	to recognize rhyming words
Sounds	to recognize alliteration, hard and soft sounds
Repetition	to recognize repeated lines and phrases.

More developed vocabulary of technical terms

Verse/stanza	to identify rhyming couplet; quatrain; sonnet; to recognize regular/irregular verse structures
Rhythm	to recognize rhythmic patterns involving stressed and unstressed syllables; to recognize rhythmic irregularities used for effect; to understand enjambment; to be able to count syllables and identify monosyllabic and polysyllabic words
Rhyme	to explain rhyme schemes in terms of *abab*
Sounds	to identify long and short vowels, hard and soft consonants, onomatopoeia, alliteration
Categories of poems	to recognize different types such as narrative poetry, love poetry, fable.

Additional sophisticated terms

Verse/stanza	to appreciate the effect of: irregularities within a regular verse structure; enjambment; line breaks/caesuras
Rhythm	to recognize how mood and tone are conveyed through regularities and irregularities of rhythm; to appreciate the effect of stressed and unstressed syllables and their patterns, such as breaking a regular pattern with consecutive stresses
Rhyme	to understand how different effects are achieved through voiced and unvoiced consonants, long and short vowels in rhymes; assonance; half rhyme
Sounds	to recognize *double entendre*; to use a range of adjectives for describing sounds, such as *mellifluous; harmonious; discordant*
Syntax of poetry	to appreciate the exploitation of prose syntax for poetic effects, such as the fronting of nouns or verbs; apostrophe/addressing the reader/exclamations; juxtaposition for effect
Repetition	to appreciate the purpose of repetition when used, for example, for emphasis; refrain; lament; celebration; humour; oral tradition
Categories of poetry	to recognize a wider range of types such as political/protest; complaint; prayer; performance/rap; reflective; lyrical.

The most important factor about these technical terms is that mere identification or labelling of features is not worthy of full credit unless it is accompanied by an analysis of their **effects**. The function of these terms is to allow students to write more succinctly and accurately.

> The way that the first line rhymes with the third line and the second line rhymes with the fourth line in each verse makes the poem...

This is a much clumsier and more time-consuming way of saying:

> The regular abab rhyme scheme makes the poem...

It is always better for students to explain the effect of a feature such as rhyme scheme in non-technical, perhaps clumsy language, than correctly identify it without any comment on its effect.

Students should use **quotation**, but it should be **brief** and **focused** and always used to **support** comments and analysis made. Copying out lines at length or quoting without analysis or comment is not worthy of credit. The most sophisticated quotation will be apt and pithy, and embedded in the body of the text.

Selection of detail and illustration in support of points and analysis is essential and needs to be **focused** and **economical**. It should *not* include re-telling or narration.

EXAMINATION TASKS

In the examination, both tiers are given a tightly focused question with three bullet points. What follows here is an illustration of the kinds of questions which will be set from 2004 onwards, with an extensive guide on the types of responses examiners will be looking for. **They are not an absolutely set pattern.**

The bullet points direct students towards a concise answer and are designed to prevent them wasting words and time on background information and general description, which so many candidates have done in the past. The sharp focus of the bullet points will make it easier for students to answer the questions **relevantly**. Many candidates failed to answer relevantly in the pre-2004 examinations, frequently because of their over-reliance on the annotation in their pre-released booklets.

Foundation

> Write about *Such is Holland!* from your pre-released booklet, and *Rider's Song* below.
>
> You must include:
> ◆ what you think is going on in *Rider's Song*
> ◆ how the writer uses language for effect in *Rider's Song*
> ◆ how the worries of the poet in *Such is Holland!* and the worries of the horseman in *Rider's Song* are different.
>
> Candidates are reminded to comment on the cultural aspects of the poems.
>
> **Such is Holland!**
> by Petrus Augustus de Genestet
> *translated by Adriaan Barnouw*
>
> O, land of mud and mist, where man is wet and shivers
> Soaked with humidity, with damp and chilly dew,
> O, land of unplumbed bogs, of roads resembling rivers,
> Land of umbrellas, gout, colds, agues, toothache, flu,
>
> O, spongy porridge-swamp, O homeland of galoshes,
> Of cobblers, toads and frogs, peat diggers, mildew, mould,
> Of ducks and every bird that slobbers, splutters, splashes,
> Hear the autumnal plaint of a poet with a cold.
>
> Thanks to your clammy clime my arteries are clotted
> With blood turned mud. No song, no joy, no peace for me.
> You're fit for clogs alone, O land our forebears plotted
> And, not at my request, extorted from the sea.

In this poem, a horseman is riding towards the city of Cordoba.

Rider's Song
by Frederico Garcia Lorca
translated from the Spanish by Alan S. Trueblood

Córdoba,
distant and lonely.

Black pony, large moon,
in my saddlebag olives.
Well as I know the roads,
I shall never reach Córdoba.

Over the plain, through the wind,
black pony, red moon.
Death keeps a watch on me
from Córdoba's towers.

Oh, such a long way to go!
And, oh, my spirited pony!
Ah, but death awaits me
before I ever reach Córdoba.

Córdoba.
Distant and lonely.

EXAM TASK *Higher*

Write a comparison of *The True Prison* from your pre-released booklet, and
Girl in the Kitchen below.

You must include:
◆ an explanation of the situation which the girl in *Girl in the Kitchen* finds
herself in
◆ reference to the effect of the poet's language in *Girl in the Kitchen*
◆ a comparison between the theme and tone of *Girl in the Kitchen* and
The True Prison.

Candidates are reminded to comment on the cultural aspects of the poems.

Ken Saro-Wiwa (1941–1995) was one of Nigeria's best-known writers. He was
a member of the Ogoni tribe, whose land has been exploited by multinational
companies extracting oil. Ken Saro-Wiwa opposed this action and the military
governments in power in Nigeria. He was arrested and charged with incitement
to murder, and was executed by hanging on 10 November 1995.

The True Prison
by Ken Saro-Wiwa

It is not the leaking roof
Nor the singing mosquitoes
In the damp, wretched cell
It is not the clank of the key

As the warden locks you in
It is not the measly rations
Unfit for beast or man
Nor yet the emptiness of day
Dipping into the blankness of night
It is not
It is not
It is not

It is the lies that have been drummed
Into your ears for a generation
It is the security agent running amok
Executing callous calamitous orders
In exchange for a wretched meal a day
The magistrate writing into her book
A punishment she knows is undeserved
The moral decrepitude
The mental ineptitude
The meat of dictators
Cowardice masking as obedience
Lurking in our denigrated souls
It is fear damping trousers
That we dare not wash
It is this
It is this
It is this
Dear friend, turns our free world
Into a dreary prison

In this poem, an Indian girl prepares food in her kitchen as an aeroplane flies
overhead.

Girl in the Kitchen
by Janaki Srinivasamurthy
translated from Kannada by A. K. Ramanujan

Like other things
they say a kitchen too
means many things
but for this girl –
this kitchen is her house
this that and every house
even the house of burial

Just as every creature
has a stomach
every house has a kitchen
I don't know whose plan it is
no windows no doors
not even a chimney for the smoke
not even a hole somewhere –
she longs for one.

As she cooks
the birds outside
the noise of playing children
buses cars autorickshaws running
into the distance
even to the seashore
but she ignores them
as she grinds the spices
renunciation comes easy, doesn't it,
when you have nothing?

Yet sometimes if she hears
the airplane in the sky
the plane! the plane! she cries
from where she is
after all what trips can she take
while she is with salt and tamarind?
the twenty-first century?
will you take me with you?
the sound in the sky
melts away
v e r y   s l o w l y

This girl in the kitchen
blows *foo foo* into the fire
and sings
maybe there's surely someone
up there in the plane
a gentleman in make-up and costume
as surely as all creatures are born
to steal and to rule

Maybe the flying chariot
will flap its wings
break through the roof
let down a ladder
lift me up as I peel potatoes
and make me the chief queen
O Rama, Rama!* carrying me
to Lanka or to Ayodhya?
old names and places
heard many times before
now what about worlds
no one has heard of?
fly to those worlds
I command you

and so on –
she weaves songs this girl
her ears open to the sounds in the sky
breaking the stalks of green chillies
her lifetime getting spent drop by drop

*The story of Rama is from the great epic of Hindu India, the *Ramayana*. Rama's rule over Ayodhya, won after mighty and fantastical battles, is the ideal of a Hindu Kingdom. The girl is calling on this mythological hero to make her his queen.

The **first bullet point** targets AO 2.1 and directs the student to the content of the unseen poem:

> 2.1 read, with insight and engagement, making appropriate references to texts and developing and sustaining interpretations of them

Students need to make a **selection** of pertinent points here without lapsing into mere description. Full answers will show **understanding, interpretation, and insight**. Students need to practice **economy** in writing responses of this kind. This is a straightforward bullet point and there are two, more demanding, bullet points to follow, so they should allocate their time sensibly.

 ◆ what you think is going on in *Rider's Song*

The weakest candidates will say that in 'Rider's Song', a man is riding his horse along the road to Cordoba. This basic, minimal response could be expanded to show a deeper understanding by explaining that the horseman is on an isolated road and he feels alone. Quoting the phrase '*distant and lonely*' to support this reading would expand the response still further. Including the colour of the horse, the saddle-bags full of olives, the '*red moon*' and the windy plain would be details which would further expand this response, showing understanding of the situation ('what is going on') in the poem.

To demonstrate interpretation and insight, candidates would need to tackle the lines '*Death keeps a watch on me*' and '*death awaits me*'. There is no 'right answer' to an interpretation of these lines, but candidates who express the idea that there is a sense of mystery, danger, of not knowing exactly what is going to happen, or why death is waiting for him in these lines, would be climbing up the mark range. Those who could express these ideas economically by using words like 'threat' and 'doom' would obviously be displaying top-level foundation skills or above.

 ◆ an explanation of the situation which the girl in *Girl in the Kitchen* finds herself in

Candidates who want to achieve the highest marks would do well to keep the explanation of the basic situation of the girl in 'Girl in the Kitchen' to an absolute minimum, i.e. that the Indian girl is preparing food in her smoky kitchen and, as an aeroplane passes overhead, she dreams about its occupants and how she might be rescued from her life of drudgery and whisked away to more exciting places. Having kept the general situation to one economical sentence, the candidate can use the rest of the response on showing the higher order skills of **interpretation** and **insight**.

By selecting brief quotation — '*the twenty-first century?*' — candidates could explain the girl's feelings of being excluded from the modern world. Details of her kitchen and her actions — such as blowing '*foo foo*' to make the fire burn; the chimney-less, windowless kitchen; the grinding of spices — could be used as evidence that she is presented as not part of the modern world symbolized by the aeroplane. Candidates would read with insight if they showed an appreciation of the contrast between the entrapment of the girl's real life, and the contrast with her fantastic imaginings. Reality is the breaking of *'the stalks of green chillies'* and the noises of birds and traffic outside; her imagination is the idea of Rama carrying her away, and of the *'flying chariot'* letting down a ladder by which she could climb to freedom in some fantasy land *'no one has heard of'*.

The **second bullet point** targets AO 2.5 and directs students to the language of the unseen poem:

> 2.5 understand and evaluate how writers use linguistic, structural, and presentational devices to achieve their effects, and comment on the ways language varies and changes

Both tiers are asked to write about the **effects** of the poet's use of language in the unseen poem. In this bullet point students are being asked to show a **discriminating** skill: to understand and **evaluate** how language (which includes sentence and verse structure if appropriate) is used to achieve effects.

Foundation candidates need to know that to comment on a writer's 'language effects', they must ask themselves **why** the writer chose these particular words/line lengths/kinds of sentences.

◆ how the writer uses language for effect in *Rider's Song*

◆ reference to the effect of the poet's language in *Girl in the Kitchen*

In preparing to answer these kinds of language bullet points, students need to consider the following:

◆ How *connotations or associative meanings* of words are used to achieve effects, such as in the 'Rider's Song', *'red moon'* suggests eeriness, mystery, or even blood in the redness, all of which link with the suggestion or threat of death. In 'Girl in the Kitchen', *'the flying chariot'* is a naïve-sounding description of an aeroplane which reflects both a mythical chariot and the unrealistic fantasizing of the girl.

◆ How *metaphorical language* is used to achieve effects. For instance, in 'Rider's Song' the personification of death in *'Death keeps a watch on me'* makes the idea or threat of death more frightening (sinister) because it sounds like a human or a creature watching the horseman from the towers of the city. In 'Girl in the Kitchen' the metaphor *'her lifetime getting spent drop by drop'*, with its suggestion of water draining away slowly, powerfully conveys the feeling of waste as the girl so full of imagination and longing must spend her time grinding spices and cutting chillies.

◆ How *culturally specific vocabulary* is used to achieve effects, such as the repetition of the name of the city *Cordoba*. This makes it sound (in ascending order of skills): more frightening and eerie; more like a threat; adds to the sense of foreboding; like a bell tolling for a death. In 'Girl in the Kitchen' the details of *'tamarind'* and *'green chillies'* place the girl in India and add to the richly sensuous appeal of the description in their appeal to sight and smell. The cry to the mythological figure in '*O Rama, Rama!*' emphasizes the wild extravagance, and the hopelessness, of the girl's fantasies.

♦ How *qualifiers, verbs forms, abstract and concrete nouns* are used for effect. In 'Rider's Song' the pair of adjectives '*distant and lonely*' is not placed before the noun it qualifies. This emphasizes the feeling of loneliness in the poem and because they are simple words with only two syllables (duosyllabic), it adds to the poem's apparent simplicity. The many nouns in 'Girl in the Kitchen' are generally unqualified, which contributes to the poem's energy and starkness and also allows the final powerful metaphor '*her lifetime getting spent drop by drop*' to stand out effectively. The only adverb in the poem, '*v e r y   s l o w l y*', also stands out. It conveys the way that the girl's dream gradually fades with the disappearing aeroplane, conveyed graphically too through the spacing which draws the words out still further.

♦ How *repetition* is used for effect. There is a great deal of repetition in the short poem 'Rider's Song', such as '*black pony, large / red moon*'. These simple words make it sound like a song, as suggested by the title. Because of the death which is waiting for the horseman, it is not a happy song. The repetition heightens this sense of impending doom. The phrase is also vivid in its visual appeal and in its suggestion of mystery. The repetition of the word '*kitchen*' throughout 'Girl in the Kitchen' places the girl very firmly in her lowly place of entrapment. The repetition of '*the plane! the plane!*' with its exclamation mark conveys the girl's wild excitement as her dreams take flight at the sight and sound of the aeroplane.

♦ Some other features which might be relevant in a consideration of language are: line length; sentence length; position of the verb in the sentence and the line; punctuation used for particular effect; rhyme used for particular effect; alliteration; enjambment; verse structure; verb tense and mood; use of personal pronouns.

The **third bullet point** targets AO 2.4:

> 2.4 select material appropriate to the purpose, collate material from different sources, and make cross references

The bullet point asks the students to show the **discriminating** skill of making cross references in comparing the unseen poem with a named pre-released poem.

This is the only opportunity for writing about the pre-released poem and students need to be economical and sharply focused in their comments and not be tempted to write down all they remember about the preparation work they have done on it.

 ♦ how the worries of the poet in *Such is Holland!* and the worries of the horseman in *Rider's Song* are different.

Candidates who say that the poet in 'Such is Holland!' is worried about the wet and mud in his country, and the horseman is worried about death are making a valid, basic comparison. This could be improved by making the comparison explicit by using a comparative connective such as 'whereas', 'on the other hand', or 'in comparison', which would help to sustain a comparison rather than giving two disparate accounts.

To climb up the mark range, candidates need to include aptly selected detail with supporting brief quotation such as: the poet is concerned about his cold which he gets from the constant wet and damp – even his '*arteries are clotted / With blood turned mud*'; he is miserable and fed up. '*No song, no joy, no peace for me*'; his ancestors had saved Holland from the sea, but it was '*not at my request*' and he wishes they had not bothered. The tone of the last is said in a jokey way (is ironic).

The worries of the horseman are much more serious in comparison: the Dutch poet is concerned just about being cold and miserable (merely about physical discomfort), whereas the horseman is afraid that death is waiting for him before he reaches Cordoba. He knows that he is alone on a deserted, wind-swept plain '*disant and lonely*' and that he will never reach his destination because '*death awaits me*'. His worries are far more serious than those of the Dutch poet.

Candidates displaying higher order skills will focus on the comparison throughout and illustrate how the Dutch poet's concerns are trivial in comparison with those of the horseman, who knows his life is threatened. A subtle point would be to sustain the comparison with reference to the tone of the two poems. The title with its exclamation mark in 'Such is Holland!' conveys a light-hearted, humorous attitude to the complaints about the Dutch climate; whereas the repetition of the statement that death is waiting for the horseman is a much more serious and dark expression of the horseman's worries.

 EXAM TASK H

◆ a comparison between the theme and tone of *Girl in the Kitchen* and *The True Prison*

For a *comparison of theme* students need to explain briefly that the two poems are 'about' similar topics. Students will expand with details of the common theme: both poems are about imprisonment. Students will display the highest order skills in explaining succinctly the different kinds of imprisonment. The girl is metaphorically imprisoned by poverty and by her status as a woman, perhaps as a daughter or household servant. Saro-Wiwa is physically imprisoned in a foetid gaol by a corrupt system where he suffers from the knowledge that he has been wrongly imprisoned, and the degrading treatment with food '*unfit for beast or man*'. His reversal of the word order in the phrase 'man or beast' to '*beast or man*' shows the extent of the degradation – human beings are made inferior to animals.

Students could subtly explore the contrast between the female, domestic theme of one and the male, political theme of the other. One is rooted firmly in India whilst the other is both specifically Nigerian, but also deliberately global and universal as expressed in the last line '*turns our free world / Into a dreary prison*'.

For a *comparison of tone* between the two poems, students should know that tone is strictly the poet's 'tone of voice', but if they include atmosphere in their analysis of tone (e.g. the atmosphere of the kitchen, the noises outside) they will receive credit. Those who focus on the tone exclusively with insightful and subtle points on the tone of the poet's voice are likely to excel. They could quote *'renunciation comes easy, doesn't it, / when you have nothing?'* as an example of the ironic tone of the **poet** which is separate from the **persona** of the girl. The poet sees the girl's life as repressed by poverty. The final line also expresses the poet's tone: *'her lifetime getting spent drop by drop'*. The girl's dreams fade as the plane disappears and the poet expresses implied criticism – clear but not harsh and judgemental – of the repression and poverty which traps her and wastes her life. The girl herself is sympathetically presented as filled with longings and dreams, but resigned to reality because she has no options.

The tone in both poems is powerful because of its emotional control and understatement. Saro-Wiwa's poem is a plea for the outside world to understand what has happened to him, and to the whole free world, as a consequence of the corruption and debasement of humankind. The tone is coolly analytical and intelligent: *'Cowardice masking as obedience / Lurking in our denigrated souls'*. The poem is powerful because the tone is not a personal complaint, but a selfless cry for the world to listen. It is addressed to *'Dear friend'*, which gives a warm tone, inviting the reader to be a universal friend. Although it is emphatic – *'It is not / It is not / It is not'* – the tone lacks aggression or hostility. The poet's argument is driven by reason and intellect, not by emotion and force, and this gives the poem its effectiveness. His tone is non-judgemental. He does not make judgements on, for example, *'The magistrate writing into her book / A punishment she knows is undeserved'*. He leaves the reader to make his or her own judgements.

BRAINSTORMED POEMS

The following poems are presented as examples of the brainstorming work that can be performed in class. Each poem is also supplied as a photocopy master for classroom use.

'Rainbow' by John Agard and 'Georgetown Children' by Ian McDonald are suggested for use with the less able. 'The Last Drive' by E. A. Brininstool and 'The True Prison' by Ken Saro-Wiwa are suitable for the more able.

John Agard has published many poetry collections for children and adults and has performed his poetry in Singapore, Canada, Germany, and Holland as well as the West Indies and Britain. Born in Guyana in 1949, he came to Britain in 1977 when he helped to form the new West Indian–British scene of jazz, dance, carnival, song, and confrontation politics. He describes his performing style as 'poetsonian', a link with the 'folksy surrealism' of the calypsonian which can be seen in this poem. Agard likes to subvert the expectations of audiences and put theatre into his poetry.

Ribbon

Rainbow
by John Agard

Why are the lines so short?
Write it out as prose putting in conventional punctuation.
What are the differences?

Caribbean English:
definite article (the) is 'de'. Other examples of Caribbean English?
Syntax (word order)?
Verbs?
What feel does it give the poem?

When you see
de rainbow
you know
God know
wha he doing –
one big smile
across the sky –
I tell you
God got style
the man got style

This address to the reader is repeated.
Where? Why?

How does the poem
make you feel?

Mood
Is it:
  celebratory
  joyful
  admiring
  humorous?

When you see
raincloud pass
and de rainbow
make a show
I tell you
is God doing
limbo
the man doing
limbo

Analyse the humour in the image of God as limbo dancer. What is the poet trying to do? (Use the information in an introductory paragraph.) Is it shocking? Funny? Does it make you think about a rainbow in a different way? How?

Punctuation
How much is there? What's missing? Why? The lies flow together (enjambment) – why is this appropriate and effective for a poem about a rainbow?

But sometimes
you know
when I see
de rainbow
so full of glow
and curving
like she bearing child
I does want to know
if God
ain't a woman

Simple vocabulary
How many one- and two-syllable words? How many with more than two syllables? What is the effect?

Repetition
How many examples? What is the effect? How well do you think this poem would go with music? What kind of music would be best?

If that is so
the woman got style
man she got style

For cross-reference and comparison
The function of natural description: 'The Last Drive'
How the poets feel about the weather: 'Such is Holland!'
Verse structure: 'just in case'

Rainbow

by John Agard

When you see
de rainbow
you know
God know
wha he doing –
one big smile
across the sky –
I tell you
God got style
the man got style

When you see
raincloud pass
and de rainbow
make a show
I tell you
is God doing
limbo
the man doing
limbo

But sometimes
you know
when I see
de rainbow
so full of glow
and curving
like she bearing child
I does want to know
if God
ain't a woman

If that is so
the woman got style
man she got style

From *Mangoes and Bullets: Selected and New Poems 1972-1984* (Pluto Press, 1985),
reproduced by permission of the author, c/o Caroline Sheldon Literary Agency

Ian McDonald is from Guyana. He has written volumes of poetry about Caribbean life. Many are about Caribbean people, such as 'Pineapple Woman', 'Rumshop Girl', and here in 'Georgetown Children', schoolchildren playing skipping games in the playground. His deceptively simple poetry conveys all the vivid colour and liveliness of the Caribbean, but it also records the harsh and the painful. Georgetown is the capital of Guyana.

Georgetown Children
by Ian McDonald

How do these lines set the poem in a particular place?

Under the soursop silver-leaf tree
The High School children play skip-and-free

Sun burning down like a fire ball
Watch the children before school call

Effect of this simile?

How does the rhythm suggest the game which the children are playing?

How do these lines create a carefree atmosphere?

Laugh in their gay time, laughter rich
Jump the jack, bring marble pitch

Black child, yellow child, brown child, white
They all the same if you looking right

Why is this syntax (grammar, word order) different from standard English?

Pass by any schoolyard in Georgetown at all
And watch the children before school call

Interpret this couplet

Under the soursop silver-leaf tree
The High School children play skip-and-free.

The biggest thing in life could be
Watching the children play skip-and-free.

Interpret this final couplet

Describe the visual image in your mind's eye from reading this poem

Verse structure
In rhyming couplets – explain and link to the topic of the poem
Rhyming words – hard or soft? Vowels short or long? Link to mood

How does the poem move from the literal to the message of the poem?

Mood
cheerful
celebratory – which words suggest this?
any suggestion of a darker mood?
reflective

Explain the use of repetition. How many examples can you find?

Sometimes, simple words can hide deeper meaning. Is it true here in this poem?

Explain whether the vocabulary is simple or complex

Do you think the poet's mood changes from the first few lines to the end?

Georgetown Children
by Ian McDonald

Under the soursop silver-leaf tree
The High School children play skip-and-free

Sun burning down like a fire ball
Watch the children before school call

Laugh in their gay time, laughter rich
Jump the jack, bring marble pitch

Black child, yellow child, brown child, white
They all the same if you looking right

Pass by any schoolyard in Georgetown at all
And watch the children before school call

Under the soursop silver-leaf tree
The High School children play skip-and-free.

The biggest thing in life could be
Watching the children play skip-and-free.

From *Jaffo the Calypsonian* (Peepal Tree, 1994),
reproduced by permission of the publisher

Mood
Consider:
reflective
nostalgic
romantic

The heyday of cowboys of the American Southwest was between the 1820s and the 1890s. The cowboy's life involved long, hard hours from before dawn to after sundown in the saddle, frequently alone on the range. Poetry and songs have been handed down from groups gathered around campfires, entertaining one another with stories, keeping alive their camaraderie.

Purpose
Consider:
to glorify?
to idealize?
to romanticize?
to portray realistically?

How is the energy in this image conveyed?

For cross-reference Compare landscape and nature with:
'Once in a Lifetime, Snow' ; 'Such is Holland'; 'Rainbow' Compare portrayal of love with:
'just in case'; 'On Going into the Province ...'

Analyse sensuous imagery in this stanza and the contrast between night and day

Why not 'sleep'?

Explain colour and movement here

Interpret the final two lines – how to do they contribute to mood and atmosphere?

The Last Drive
by E. A. Brininstool

Metaphorical significance of title?

Verse structure
Is the decasyllabic line regular? How could the pattern be seen as appropriate? Effect of stress falling on final word in each line?

Is this a stereotype? A cliché? Are there any similar?

Why this archaic language? Find other examples. Effect?

How is the camaraderie between the cowboys shown here and elsewhere?

Effect of this choice of vocabulary?

What effect is intended in this line?

Effect of this alliteration? Refer to other examples.

How does this description of the stream contribute to the mood of the poem?

Connotations of this phrase? What is the reader meant to feel for the old cowboy? How far is it successful with you?

Beside his sagging door he sits and smokes,
And dreams again of old trail days, long gone.
His eyes are dim; his form is bent and old,
And silvered are the locks about his brow.
He hears again the thud of pony-hoofs,
The clash of horns, the bellowing of herds;
The shout of riders and the pant of steeds,
And creak of saddle-leather as they ride.
He sees the dust-clouds hover o'er the trail
Where, snaky-like, the herd winds on and on;
He sees broad-hatted men, bronzed, fearless, bold,
And as he listens, faintly to his ears
Is borne the echoes of an old trail song,
While to his nostrils floats the scent of sage
And greasewood, cactus and mesquite, that seems
To lure him back among his ranges wide.

'Tis night! And now he sees the bedded herd
Beneath the studded canopy of heaven,
While hardy night-guards keep their vigil drear.
The stars gleam out, and yonder rocky buttes
Loom strange and weird and dim and spectral-like;
The wagon top shines brightly by the stream,
And in the flickering campfire's feeble glow
He sees the silent forms of old range pals
In dreamless slumber in their blanket beds.
The coyote's melancholy wail floats in
Upon the silent, pulseless summer air,
While overhead, on steady, tireless wing,
The night-hawk whirls and circles in its flight,
And down below, the babble of the stream
Makes low-crooned, soothing music rippling by.
Morn comes, with crimson bars of light that leap
To gild the buttes and tint the east with fire;
The lark's song echoes clear and sweet and strong
Upon the morning air; the range-grass gleams
And glitters with its diamond-tinted dew,
And all the great wide prairie springs to life.

Again he sees the straggling herd move on
In broken line, and in his dreams he seems
To feel the bronco's tireless, steady pace
That carries him upon his last long drive
Which ends in sleep along the Sunset Trail.

The Last Drive
by E. A. Brininstool

Beside his sagging door he sits and smokes,
And dreams again of old trail days, long gone.
His eyes are dim; his form is bent and old,
And silvered are the locks about his brow.
He hears again the thud of pony-hoofs,
The clash of horns, the bellowing of herds;
The shout of riders and the pant of steeds,
And creak of saddle-leather as they ride.
He sees the dust-clouds hover o'er the trail
Where, snaky-like, the herd winds on and on;
He sees broad-hatted men, bronzed, fearless, bold,
And as he listens, faintly to his ears
Is borne the echoes of an old trail song,
While to his nostrils floats the scent of sage
And greasewood, cactus and mesquite, that seems
To lure him back among his ranges wide.

'Tis night! And now he sees the bedded herd
Beneath the studded canopy of heaven,
While hardy night-guards keep their vigil drear.
The stars gleam out, and yonder rocky buttes
Loom strange and weird and dim and spectral-like;
The wagon top shines brightly by the stream,
And in the flickering campfire's feeble glow
He sees the silent forms of old range pals
In dreamless slumber in their blanket beds.
The coyote's melancholy wail floats in
Upon the silent, pulseless summer air,
While overhead, on steady, tireless wing,
The night-hawk whirls and circles in its flight,
And down below, the babble of the stream
Makes low-crooned, soothing music rippling by.
Morn comes, with crimson bars of light that leap
To gild the buttes and tint the east with fire;
The lark's song echoes clear and sweet and strong
Upon the morning air; the range-grass gleams
And glitters with its diamond-tinted dew,
And all the great wide prairie springs to life.

Again he sees the straggling herd move on
In broken line, and in his dreams he seems
To feel the bronco's tireless, steady pace
That carries him upon his last long drive
Which ends in sleep along the Sunset Trail.

From *Cowboy Poetry* edited by Julie Saffel
(Castle Books, 2001)

Ken Saro-Wiwa (1941–1995) was one of Nigeria's best-known writers. He was a member of the Ogoni tribe, whose land has been exploited by multinational companies extracting oil. Ken Saro-Wiwa opposed this action and the military governments in power in Nigeria. He was arrested and charged with incitement to murder, and was executed by hanging on 10 November 1995.

What is the true prison?

Why are there no similes in this poem?

You know Saro-Wiwa was hanged unlawfully. Does this knowledge affect your reaction to the poem? Explain in what way.

Analyse this patterning. How it is repeated in the second stanza?

The True Prison
by Ken Saro-Wiwa

It is not the leaking roof
Nor the singing mosquitoes
In the damp, wretched cell
It is not the clank of the key
As the warden locks you in
It is not the measly rations
Unfit for beast or man
Nor yet the emptiness of day
Dipping into the blankness of night
It is not
It is not
It is not

What hardships does he have to suffer in prison?

Effect of adjectives in these lines?

Effect of these abstract nouns?

Connotations and effect of this choice of verb?

It is the lies that have been drummed
Into your ears for a generation
It is the security agent running amok
Executing callous calamitous orders
In exchange for a wretched meal a day
The magistrate writing into her book
A punishment she knows is undeserved
The moral decrepitude
The mental ineptitude
The meat of dictators
Cowardice masking as obedience
Lurking in our denigrated souls
It is fear damping trousers
That we dare not wash
It is this
It is this
It is this
Dear friend, turns our free world
Into a dreary prison

Double entendre?

Effect of hard consonants in these adjectives?

Interpret – analyse tone and sounds of words

Connotations of these participles? Interpret

Who is the audience?

Analyse metaphorical sense

Purpose
consider:
political
protest
reform
justice

Tone
consider:
restraint?
understatement?
emotions?
anger?

Pace
Analyse how the climax is arrived at

Theme
imprisonment?
corruption?

For cross-reference and comparison
Other kinds of imprisonment:
'Girl in the Kitchen'
'A Blindman Sings'
Contrast mood – reality v. romantic:
'The Last Drive'
Thoughts on freedom:
'Georgetown Children'

The True Prison
by Ken Saro-Wiwa

It is not the leaking roof
Nor the singing mosquitoes
In the damp, wretched cell
It is not the clank of the key
As the warden locks you in
It is not the measly rations
Unfit for beast or man
Nor yet the emptiness of day
Dipping into the blankness of night
It is not
It is not
It is not

It is the lies that have been drummed
Into your ears for a generation
It is the security agent running amok
Executing callous calamitous orders
In exchange for a wretched meal a day
The magistrate writing into her book
A punishment she knows is undeserved
The moral decrepitude
The mental ineptitude
The meat of dictators
Cowardice masking as obedience
Lurking in our denigrated souls
It is fear damping trousers
That we dare not wash
It is this
It is this
It is this
Dear friend, turns our free world
Into a dreary prison

From *Captured Voices* edited by Janna Letts and Fiona Whytehead
(Victor Gollancz, 1999)

Support for
less able students

The section on pages 34–71 contains a wealth of help and stimulation for less able students. The structured guidance, illustration, explanations, and task setting in each unit are carefully designed for students to work through on their own, or with minimal teacher help. There is plenty of opportunity for them to practise basic skills and to develop higher grade skills step by step. The guidance is designed to target the assessment objectives for both Reading and Writing in the specifications, but these are expressed in clear, wholly accessible language so that students are not burdened with 'AO-speak', which they find both daunting and boring.

WRITING UNITS

◆ A: Presenting an argument in a written speech
◆ B: Writing a persuasive letter

These tasks offer step-by-step guidance in answering two examination-style writing questions, one of which was introduced in the *Student's Book*. Each starts with finding ideas for the topic and includes detailed guidance on organizing a written answer effectively at text, paragraph, and sentence level. Help is given on writing for different audiences and purposes to enable students to write their own responses to the tasks set at the end. Photocopiable planning sheets are provided for each task set.

READING TO WRITE UNITS: TEACHER-FREE!

These four units target different basic writing skills:

◆ A: *Man Bites Snake* – organizing and indenting paragraphs
◆ B: *Bringing Back the Bloodhounds* – using commas
◆ C: *Folk Story* – setting out and punctuating direct speech
◆ D: *The Storm* – identifying and using nouns, adjectives, adverbs, and personal pronouns.

These four very attractive units are **fully photocopiable** (PCMs 8–16) and designed for students to work through on their own. They could be used for the whole class, for groups, or for individuals within a class or group who would benefit from basic skills practice.

Each one begins with a simple, brief, and interesting text which has been written specifically to facilitate the learning of the targeted basic writing skill. Following each text, clear and simply expressed explanations, examples, questions, and tasks enable students to master these basic skills at their own pace without a teacher's input. The symbol ◆ guides the students through the step-by-step tasks. The paragraphing and direct speech units have self-assessment sections at the end.

READING UNITS

The texts offered here are from a variety of printed sources including autobiography, travel writing, and newspaper articles. Other features of media writing are targeted, including headlines and the text of a leaflet. They are brief and accessible, and have been chosen to appeal to both school and further education students. They illustrate effective writing for different purposes and audiences, and perhaps most importantly, they are interesting and enjoyable.

At the beginning of each unit, a **Learning Box** explains in simple language the key words and terms in the unit, such as 'puns' and 'literal and metaphorical meanings'. An **Exam Terms** box explains simply and clearly what is required by the relevant instructions, such as 'analyse' and 'convey'.

In order to give students the satisfaction of completing a task, and to encourage accuracy, precision, and care in their choice of language, they are asked to write only paragraphs or defined sections of a piece of writing, using the specific skills they have learned in the unit.

- A: *A Tale of Suffering and Misery* – from a leaflet produced by an organization protesting against the treatment of battery hens. Students are guided through an analysis of the language used to express strong opinions, encouraged to evaluate the text, and then asked to write part of their own anti-meat leaflet.
- B: *Jungle Fever* – a gruesome encounter with a minute flesh-eater in travel writing set in the Venezuelan rainforest. Students are guided to extend their understanding into interpretation, and to include accurately punctuated and correctly set out direct speech in a dramatic mini-story of their own.
- C: *Web of Deceit* – the layout features of media texts including the headline, strap-line, and picture caption from an article on Internet stalking. Students are guided through analysis of the effects of these features and asked to write their own for a different topic.
- D: *Father and I* – a brief childhood memory rich in sensuous language and palpable emotions. Students are guided through an analysis of the connotations and associations of words and asked to write a mini-account of a memory of their own.
- E: *Flying* – the terror and the facts: two media extracts enabling students to understand, analyse, and interpret contrasting purposes, layout, and effects, and to write their own contrasting paragraphs for different purposes.

You are asked to speak in your year group's debate.
The motion is:

Childhood is the best time of your life

Argue for or against the motion. Write out your speech in full.

?¿ What am I being asked to do?

You have to pretend that you are going to make a speech in a **debate**.

In a debate, a group of people discuss a topic which people disagree about. When people have different **opinions**, it means that they have different points of views or beliefs.

In a debate, the topic being discussed is called the **motion**. Those who agree with the topic **propose the motion**. Those who disagree with the topic **oppose the motion**. The people who do not agree with your opinion are called **opponents**.

Speakers in the debate give their opinions about the topic and **argue** that other people should share their opinion. Their **argument** has to be strong if they are going to succeed in persuading people to change their minds.

Argument in a debate doesn't mean 'having an argument' and getting angry with the person who doesn't share your opinion. It means making sure your opponents fully understand your opinion through the reasons you give. You have to **persuade** your opponents by the strength of those reasons. Just as important as the strength of your reasons is the way you **express** them.

You are asked to write out your speech.

?¿ How do I start?

PCM
5

First of all think about the topic.

Fill in as many reasons as you can under these headings.

Why might childhood be the best time of your life?
Because my mum and dad look after me
Because I don't have to go to work …

*Why might childhood **not** be the best time of your life?*
Because I might not have a good home
Because I might hate primary school …

?¿ I've a list of reasons, now what?

You have found plenty of reasons for both sides of the argument. Now decide which side you are going to argue for. Are you **for the motion** (do you think childhood *is* the best time of your life)? Or are you **against the motion** (do you think childhood *is not* the best time of your life)? There is no right or wrong answer. It just depends on your point of view.

⟦?¿⟧ I don't think childhood is the best time! I'm going to argue against the motion.

Go back to your list of reasons. You may have reasons such as:

> I was always in trouble at primary school
> I used to cry myself to sleep because of all the tests we had and I couldn't do them
> My dad left when I was three and my mum had to work weekends

These reasons are all good reasons why *your* childhood was not the best time of your life. They are **personal** reasons.

In a piece of writing like this, it won't be **appropriate** (what is required by the question) to describe *just* your personal experiences.

What you need to do is to widen your ideas from personal experience only, and think about the **issues** involved in the question topic. This means thinking about childhood in general and what does, or doesn't, make it the best time.

Go back to your reasons and make general points about children and childhood, and not about yourself. When you write your general points, don't use the personal pronoun 'I'.

Making a personal point —
> I was always in trouble at primary school
> I used to cry myself to sleep because of all the tests we had and I couldn't do them

Making a general point —
> Primary school is often a time of unhappiness to children. They can feel picked on by teachers and they can find tests frightening.

⟦?¿⟧ So what do I do with my personal experience points?

Personal experience can be used to **illustrate** your general point in an interesting way. It will make your point more powerful and will appeal to your audience.

General point —
> Primary school is often a time of unhappiness to children. They can feel picked on by teachers and they can find tests frightening.

Using personal experience for illustration —
> Primary school is often a time of unhappiness to children. They can feel picked on by teachers and they can find tests frightening. I can remember crying myself to sleep over the maths test we had on Mondays with terrifying Mr Garett.

Make more points and illustrate them with your personal experience, using this as a guide.

?¿ I've made my illustrated points. What do I do with them?

Paragraphs are very important in your writing. They make your argument orderly and more powerful. You should aim to write three paragraphs.

Arrange your general points under three paragraph headings:

1 Unhappiness at school
2 Difficult home background
3 Lack of independence

?¿ How do I make my general points 'speech-like'?

You're not just writing an opinion essay, you're writing a speech. You have to show that you know you're writing for a particular **purpose** and **audience**.

Remember, you want to:
◆ persuade your audience
◆ catch their attention
◆ hold their attention.

One way of doing this is to ask the audience **provocative questions**. A provocative question is one that stirs up your audience and makes them *feel* an emotion like anger or sympathy.

Go back to the general point you made above:

> Primary school is often a time of unhappiness to children. They can feel picked on by teachers and they can find tests frightening. I can remember crying myself to sleep over the maths test we had on Mondays with terrifying Mr Garett.

Add a comment or two including a question directed to your audience:

> I bet you can all think of similar miserable memories of school. Do you think this makes a happy childhood?

To be even more effective, you could write a *really* provocative question which would stir up your audience even more:

> Do you really believe that fear and misery makes a happy childhood? I certainly do not!

PCM
6

This makes your point powerfully. Use a question like this in each of your paragraphs. Don't forget the question mark!

?¿ How do I start my speech?

There are various ways of starting a speech.

The **formal** way in a **formal** debate is to start:

> Madam (or Mr) Chairman, Ladies and Gentlemen, I am going to speak
> in favour of (or against) the motion today.

You can start more **informally**:

> Good Morning, Class, I am going to ...
> Good Morning, Year Group, I am going to...

Whichever way you choose, make sure you get the commas in the right place and that you spell the words correctly.

The simplest way to end your speech is:

> Thank you for listening today.

Don't sign your name at the end.

?¿ I have problems with my full stops. What's the best way to check them?

Go back over your writing. Each sentence that you have written should make a point. When the point has been made, check that there is a full stop.

Try reading it out loud – or, in an exam, pretend you are reading it out loud. When you need to pause and breathe in, you need a full stop.

Check that the letter which begins the next sentence after the full stop is a *capital letter*.

When you write your capital letters, make sure you write them correctly. Your capital letters must look different from your small (**lower case**) letters. Check particularly for F (capital) and f (lower case); J and j. Make sure that your capital letters are on the line and are taller than your lower case letters.

If you don't do this, your handwriting will make it look to an examiner as if you don't know how to use capital letters.

?¿ What about commas?

The most important thing about commas is that they should *not* be used instead of full stops. When you check for your full stops, you will find that you change some commas to full stops.

Commas are to show a brief pause which separates some words from the main sentence:

> Some teachers, fortunately not many, are terrifying to young children.
> Most parents look after their children with love and care, but some do not.

Remember, it is better to leave commas out rather than put them in where they break up the sense of what you are writing.

?¿ Is there any other punctuation I should check?

Yes, questions marks!

Asking questions in your speech is an **effective** way of making your points, but don't forget the question marks. Check to make sure they are there and that the letter beginning the following sentence is a capital letter.

Remember, a question mark stands on its own – never add a full stop as well.

> I'd much rather have my independence than rely on my parents for everything, wouldn't you?

?¿ How can I improve my vocabulary?

1   Go back over your writing. Look for dull or ugly words like *get, got, nice, good, bad*. Cross them out and over the top write a much more interesting and lively word.

> recovers from
> Sometimes a child never ~~gets over~~ the disappearance of a parent.
> deprived / tragic / unhappy
> Some childhoods are really ~~bad~~.

2   Use some **adjectives** and **adverbs** to add interest and life to your writing. Use an omission mark ⋏ and write in your adjective or adverb.

> Adjectives: beloved/much loved/adored/favourite
> Sometimes a child never recovers from the disappearance of a ⋏ parent.
>
> Adverbs: absolutely/totally/exclusively
> Young children have to rely ⋏ on whoever is looking after them.

?¿ Does spelling really matter?

Yes – but spelling some words wrongly matters more than spelling others wrongly!

Don't let spelling stop you using interesting words. It's always better to write *glorious, superb, successful* or *sympathetic* and spell it wrongly, than to use *good* because you are confident that you can spell it correctly.

Words you *must* spell correctly are:
✔ words given in the question, e.g. *argue; motion*
✔ words in everyday use, e.g. *father; because; somewhere; believe*
✔ **negative verbs** with apostrophes, e.g. *can't; doesn't; won't*
✔ pairs of words which are often confused, e.g. *where / were; lose / loose; your / you're; to / too*
✔ The endings of verbs in the past tense that end in *-ed*, e.g. *answered*.

BRAINSTORMING YOUR TOPIC

'Childhood is the best time of your life'

Why might childhood be the best time of your life?

Because my mum and dad look after me

Because I don't have to go to work

Why might childhood not be the best time of your life?

Because I might not have a good home

Because I might hate primary school

PLANNING SHEET

'Childhood is the best time of your life'

IDEAS

For the motion	Against the motion

Introduction

Main arguments

Questions to ask the audience

Conclusion

Task from the *Students' Book*, page 83

A youth leader is running an outdoors activity week in the Lake District, where there will be a wide choice of activities, including rock climbing, abseiling, and horse riding. He has advertised in your local paper for young people to apply for one *free* place on the trip. Write a letter to the youth leader to try to persuade him to choose *you* for the free place.

?¿ What am I being asked to do?

You are being asked to write a persuasive letter to a youth leader offering a free place on an activity week. When he reads your letter, he has to think 'Wow! This young person *must* have that free place!'

It's your job to make the youth leader feel that way. You have to **persuade** him that you're the one.

?¿ How do I lay out a letter like this?

This isn't a letter to a friend or someone you know, it is a **formal letter**. There are rules for laying out a formal letter which you must follow.

You must include:
◆ your address
◆ the title of the person to whom you are writing (the 'addressee')
◆ the addressee's address
◆ the date
◆ a salutation (e.g. Dear Sir)
◆ a signing off (e.g. Yours faithfully)
◆ your signature
◆ your name with Mr/Mrs/Miss/Ms printed underneath

You have a choice of layout:
a) as in a word-processed letter, or
b) as in a handwritten letter.

Depending on the question you are asked, you will probably have to make up some of the details on the letter layout, such as someone's name. Here, you have to make up the name and address of the local newspaper in which the advertisement appeared.

Word-processed letter

The easiest way is to block everything down the left-hand margin with no punctuation at all, like this:

Rosehurst
4 Orchard Close
Oldbury
Gloucestershire GL3 7GK

The Youth Leader
The Oldbury Echo
12 High Street
Oldbury
Gloucestershire GL3 4BN

June 12th 2002

Dear Mr Arrowhead

[And at the end of your letter:]

Yours sincerely

Sarah Manners

Miss Sarah Manners

Handwritten letter

You need to include the same information but you lay it out differently and you punctuate with commas and full stops.

Rosehurst,
4, Orchard Close,
Oldbury,
Gloucestershire GL3 7GK.

June 12th 2002

The Youth Leader,
The Oldbury Echo,
12 High Street,
Oldbury,
Gloucestershire GL3 4BN.

Dear Mr Arrowhead,

[And at the end of your letter:]

Yours sincerely,

Sarah Manners

Miss Sarah Manners

?¿ How do I start?

In your first paragraph state the **purpose** of your letter – that is, say why you are writing. Keep it brief and absolutely clear. Tell the youth leader in two sentences that:

1. you have seen his advertisement in *The Oldbury Echo* (or whatever you have called your local newspaper)
2. you want him to consider you for the free place on the activity week.
   - ◆ Indent your paragraph (that means start a little way in from the left margin).
   - ◆ Check your full stops!

?¿ Then what?

Pick one of the activities that you'd really like to do, like abseiling. **Organize** your thoughts and ideas into a plan.

This letter needs about three more paragraphs after your first brief introductory paragraph.
- ◆ In paragraph 1, express your longing to try abseiling.
- ◆ In paragraph 2, describe persuasively how fantastic you imagine abseiling would be.
- ◆ In paragraph 3, give persuasive, personal reasons why you should be chosen.

?¿ I've said I want to go abseiling, but it sounds a bit boring.

If you've written something like this:

> I would really like to go abseiling. It would be really exciting.

… your meaning is clear, but it won't make the youth leader give you a free place. He wants to see energy and enthusiasm in your words.

So think of different, **vivid** words, expressions and phrases to describe how much you'd like to abseil and how exciting you would find it.

absolutely
    adore
      ambition
        heartfelt
         challenging
         extreme sport
         tremendously
       love
        dream
         fantasy
          clouds
           adrenalin
           hugely
             desire
             lifelong
              adventure   *wildest*   *high*

PCM 7

Using different coloured highlighters for each, identify these words as nouns, adjectives, verbs or adverbs. Match them together, using other exciting words you can think of, to make **lively**, **punchy** phrases (a punchy phrase is one that hits you with its energy, liveliness or wit).

Use these punchy phrases to write three sentences in which you express your enormous desire to try abseiling. Make your first sentence a short, **simple** sentence. Make your two other sentences **complex** (complex sentences have different clauses).

Simple sentence:

> I would absolutely love to go abseiling.

Complex sentence:

> I would absolutely love to go abseiling <u>because</u> ever since I watched an abseiling display when I was eight years old, I have dreamed of being able to take part in such a challenging extreme sport.

Look at the use of the **connective** (or **connecting word**) *because*. This joins two sentences together.

Two sentences with two full stops:

> I would absolutely love to go abseiling. Ever since I watched an abseiling display when I was eight years old, I have dreamed of being able to take part in such a challenging extreme sport.

One sentence with one final full stop and one connecting word, *because:*

> I would absolutely love to go abseiling <u>because</u> ever since I watched an abseiling display when I was eight years old, I have dreamed of being able to take part in such a challenging extreme sport.

Use connectives in your complex sentences. Some other connectives are: *and; although; before; if; until; whether.*

If you add a clause to the main sentence, you must mark it off with a comma. Main sentence:

> I have dreamed of being able to take part in such a challenging extreme sport.

Add a clause, and remember the comma:

> Ever since I watched an abseiling display when I was eight years old, I have dreamed of being able to take part in such a challenging extreme sport.

Use a comma in this way in at least one of your three sentences.

?¿ In my next paragraph, how do I write the description?

To describe how fantastic it would be to abseil, write at least one complex sentence on each of the following:

1   Imagine what it would feel like physically (that is, the wind against your face and so on).
2   How would you feel emotionally, during and after the experience (a mixture of terror and exhilaration, perhaps)?
3   What would you see from your bird's eye position?

Think about how you could use the following words. Use a dictionary to look up any you don't know. Make sure you spell them correctly!

freedom

air currents
riding
soaring
flying
wings

the elements
gusts of wind
achievement
challenge
solitary
free fall
fulfilment

to fulfil a dream
fulfilling
escapism
ultimate

Make your description even more enthusiastic by using some **superlatives**. The superlative form of an adjective is the one which means 'the most'. Here are some examples:

Adjective	Superlative form
great	greatest
wild	wildest
challenging	most challenging
exhilarating	most exhilarating
invigorating	most invigorating

?¿ Will my description persuade the youth leader?

Your enthusiasm and strong desire will come through your description, and that will persuade the youth leader. To conclude your paragraph with some powerful persuasion, add a sentence directed to the youth leader which is **explicitly** persuasive (**explicit** means clearly stated).

> This is my wildest dream and only you have the power to make it come true for me.

This is an example. Write your own persuasive sentence.

[?¿] What sort of personal reasons should I use to persuade in my last paragraph?

The most appropriate and persuasive reasons in this question would be to do with money. There could be illness or redundancy in your family which means you could never hope to go on an activity week unless you won the free place. Perhaps you had a week booked last year, but had to pull out because your father had an accident and was off work. Perhaps you have never had a real holiday because your family can't afford it. But don't exaggerate your hard luck here. More than one family tragedy is just too much to believe! Perhaps it would be the break you need to get started on a course you plan to do after GCSEs …

Whatever reasons you choose, include some **persuasive phrases** and **clauses** in your sentences such as:

> This is my only chance of a life experience …
> It would be a unique opportunity for me to …
> What a fantastic experience it would be …
> Please would you consider …

[?¿] How do I finish off?

Finish with one or two simple sentences. You could end with just:

> Please choose me!

A more effective ending might be a little longer. Note the comma, the exclamation mark and the final full stop:

> If you chose me, I would be the happiest young person in the world! I do hope you will.

Then sign off, according to the layout plan you have used:
◆ If you started *Dear Mr X*, finish with *Yours sincerely*
  If you started *Dear Sir*, finish with *Yours faithfully*

Note the capital Y and the spelling of *sincerely* and *faithfully*.

PLANNING A LETTER OF PERSUASION

Information to include:
Your address

The title of the person to whom you are writing (the 'addressee')

The addressee's address

The date   A salutation (e.g. Dear Sir)

A signing off (e.g. Yours faithfully)   Your signature

Your name with Mr/Mrs/Miss/Ms printed underneath

Introductory paragraph

Main paragraph 1 Express your longing to try abseiling

Main paragraph 2 Describe persuasively how fantastic you imagine abseiling would be

Main paragraph 3 Give persuasive, personal reasons why you should be chosen

Concluding persuasive sentence:

Read through the following. This story, or narrative account, is true.

Man Bites Snake. A South African man bit his way to freedom after he was attacked by a python in 2002. Lucas Sibanda, aged 53, was walking along the road near his home on his way to the food-processing factory where he worked. He spotted the snake in the grass bank close to him and was so terrified that he could not move. Lucas spoke of his experience later. 'I froze for almost ten seconds,' he said. 'And that gave the python all the time it needed.' South Africans are quite rightly frightened of the deadly python which is a native of their country. Pythons are constrictors. They kill animals and human beings by wrapping themselves tightly around their prey so that it cannot break free. To be attacked by a python is a truly terrifying, and usually fatal, experience. In seconds, Lucas found the python tangled tightly around him. He knew immediately that the python would kill him within minutes. There was only one way to survive. 'I decided there was only one way to save myself from the monster,' Lucas explained. 'And that was to bite it just below its head.' He sank his teeth repeatedly into the python and kicked and punched it until it released its grip. Finally, as it lay on the ground, he killed it with a stick.

Organizing your paragraphs

Your task is to write out this text in three paragraphs, as follows.

Paragraph 1: introduction/background
Paragraph 2: the beginning of the narrative account
Paragraph 3: the conclusion of the narrative account.

You will need to rearrange the text.

❖ To find your first paragraph, highlight the lines in the middle of the text which you think would make a suitable introduction to the account.

❖ In the middle of the narrative account, find the line which you think makes a good break in the story.

❖ End your second paragraph at this break, and begin your third paragraph after it.

Indenting your paragraphs

❖ Indent each paragraph. This means start each new paragraph at least a centimetre in from the left-hand margin.

❖ Start with a capital letter.

Setting out the direct speech

❖ Direct speech needs a new line.

❖ Open the speech marks against the left-hand margin.

❖ After the direct speech has finished, start the next line against the left-hand margin.

Writing the title or heading

❖ Write the title either in the centre of the line or against the left-hand margin.

❖ Leave a line clear underneath the title.

Writing clearly

Make sure your handwriting is legible.

❖ Form your letters correctly – don't let some letters get 'swallowed up' by others.

❖ Make sure your capital letters and small letters are quite different, and place them correctly on the line – look particularly at F/f, J/j, P/p, G/g, and L/l.

❖ Make sure every new sentence has a capital letter, correctly formed.

This is how the text could be written. Check yours against it.

Man Bites Snake

South Africans are quite rightly frightened of the deadly python which is a native of their country. Pythons are constrictors. They kill animals and human beings by wrapping themselves tightly around their prey so that it cannot break free. To be attacked by a python is a truly terrifying, and usually fatal, experience.

A South African man bit his way to freedom after he was attacked by a python in 2002. Lucas Sibanda, aged 53, was walking along the road near his home on his way to the food-processing factory where he worked. He spotted the snake in the grass bank close to him and was so terrified that he could not move. Lucas spoke of his experience later.

'I froze for almost ten seconds,' he said. 'And that gave the python all the time it needed.' In seconds, Lucas found himself with the python tangled tightly around him.

He knew immediately that the python would kill him within minutes. There was only one way to survive.

'I decided there was only one way to save myself from the monster,' Lucas explained. 'And that was to bite it just below its head.' He sank his teeth repeatedly into the python and kicked and punched it until it released its grip. Finally, as it lay on the ground, he killed it with a stick.

Read the following text:

Bringing Back the Bloodhounds

In today's age of DNA testing and electronic surveillance, the police have discovered that in some cases the best equipment that money can buy has four legs, long ears and very floppy skin … a bloodhound. Two bloodhounds, Morse and Sherlock, are already working with Essex police and fifteen other forces are considering introducing them.

When hunting missing persons or criminals, German Shepherd dogs can follow trails which are up to 48 hours old. Bloodhounds, on the other hand, can follow trails a great deal older. This is because, unlike other dogs, they catch the scent in the air as well as on the ground. 'Sherlock followed a trail which was thirteen days old,' said the head of dog training at Essex police. 'He followed the trail down several roads and finally identified the thief's house even though the man had driven home by car.'

Bloodhounds do have their downside, undoubtedly. Morse, eighteen months old, had to have surgery to remove an excess flap of skin from above his eye to his throat which was obscuring his vision. Even with full sight, the dogs are not aggressive hunters. Once on the trail, however, they are transformed. 'They will go for hours,' said a police-dog trainer from Cornwall. 'They get so absorbed that you have to stop them crashing into trees, parked cars or lamp-posts.'

Then there are those loose, hanging folds of skin. The folds create a sling effect and a single shake of the bloodhound's head can fling saliva up to twenty feet!

Commas have functions. In this text, you can see some of their different functions.

Parenthetical commas

These are commas which go before and after a group of words which add something to a sentence. The words give you a bit more information, but the sentence would still be a sentence without them.

Morse, eighteen months old, had to have surgery.

Morse had to have surgery is the main sentence. The phrase *eighteen months old* tells you a bit more about him. This phrase therefore has commas around it.

◆ Find another example in the text of parenthetical commas like these. Write it down.

◆ Write two sentences of your own using commas in this way.

Words which add a comment

Commas are used to mark off words such as:

on the other hand; to be honest; as a matter of fact; I suppose; undoubtedly; quite

frankly; fortunately; as you know; first of all; however; personally

How the commas are used depends on the position of the words in the sentence. Look at the following sentence:

Beckham is the best player England has had for a long time.

We can add the comment words *to be honest,* punctuated with commas:

Beckham is, to be honest, the best player England has had for a long time.

To be honest, Beckham is the best player England has had for a long time.

Beckham is the best player England has had for a long time, to be honest.

In the text, a comment word is seen in:

Bloodhounds do have their downside, undoubtedly.

The comment word is *undoubtedly.*

◆ Find another example in the text of comment words punctuated with a comma or commas. Write it down.

◆ Write two sentences of your own using comment words correctly punctuated with commas.

Commas following a clause or phrase

Clauses and phrases add information and interest to a sentence. At the beginning of a sentence, they are punctuated with commas.

Here is the main sentence:

German Shepherd dogs can follow trails which are up to 48 hours old.

Here is the phrase:

when hunting missing persons or criminals

Here is the complete sentence with the phrase punctuated with a comma:

When hunting missing persons or criminals, German Shepherd dogs can follow trails which are up to 48 hours old.

◆ Find another sentence in the text containing a phrase or clause punctuated in this way. Write down the whole sentence.

◆ Write two sentences of your own containing phrases or clauses punctuated in this way.

Using commas in lists

When more than one element is listed in a sentence, the elements are separated by a comma.

It has four legs, long ears and very floppy skin.

If you add more elements, you add commas:

It has four legs, a drooling mouth, long ears, soft fur and very floppy skin.

You do not need a comma at the end of the list before the *and.*

◆ Find another example of a list with a comma from the text. Write it down.

◆ Write two sentences of your own using a list with commas.

Writing tag questions

A tag is the little tail which is often put on the end of a statement, particularly when we speak:

Statement:

It was a terrifying ride.

Question:

It was a terrifying ride, wasn't it?

Wasn't it? is the tag which makes the statement into a question.

Write some tag questions using the text. Here are some examples:

The police bloodhounds are called Morse and Sherlock, aren't they?

Criminals can be found by bloodhounds, can't they?

◆ Now write five tag questions of your own using the text.

Note carefully:

✔ Include a comma before your tag.

✔ Put a question mark at the end of your question.

✔ Put the apostrophe in the right place in your tag verb, e.g. *won't; isn't; couldn't.*

Read this folk story.

Paragraph 1 In a distant country many years ago, there lived a boy, Hando, and his grandfather. Times were hard. There had been three poor harvests in three successive years and many people in the village had died from lack of food. Grandfather Jan did whatever work he could to earn just enough to buy rice and, sometimes, vegetables to keep Hando and himself alive. **Paragraph 2** One day, Hando could hardly believe his eyes. Grandfather Jan was walking towards their hut carrying a large piece of pork. Grandfather! cried Hando excitedly as his grandfather came in. We *never* have meat! Are we going to have a celebration? Perhaps we are, Grandfather Jan replied, but he wasn't smiling. **Paragraph 3** Hando felt a burning hunger in his stomach as he watched his grandfather prepare the pork. Why are you putting salt all over it, Grandfather? he asked, puzzled. Why aren't you slicing it for the frying pan? You'll see, my boy, was his reply. Hando could tell that this was the only answer he would get from his grandfather, so he waited patiently until suppertime, a ravenous hunger gnawing his insides. **Paragraph 4** At last, Grandfather Jan set two bowls of plain rice on the table as usual and called Hando to eat. Above the table, out of reach, hung the piece of pork preserved in its salty casing. Hando looked at it, open-mouthed. Have another piece, boy, said his grandfather. Doesn't it taste good? But I haven't got any! Hando cried, frustrated and uncomprehending. Just taste it, continued the old man. But Grandfather, Hando cried again, feeling tears pricking his eyes. You haven't given me any! Grandfather Jan looked at his grandson with a fond smile. If you think about it long enough, boy, you'll taste it alright, he said. **Paragraph 5** And so, each day after that, Hando and his grandfather ate their plain rice beneath the hanging salted pork.

Highlighting the speech

In this story there are two characters:

◆ Grandfather Jan

◆ The boy, Hando

Your task is to write it out, setting out the direct speech correctly.

◆ Use one colour to highlight the grandfather's words, and another colour to highlight the boy's words.

◆ Use a third colour to highlight the words such as *Hando cried again, feeling tears pricking his eyes* or *continued the old man*, which tell you who spoke the words.

Setting out the direct speech

◆ Direct speech needs a new line.

◆ Put opening speech marks against the left-hand margin.

◆ After the direct speech has finished, start the next line against the left-hand margin.

> '*I wish I could have some of that pork,*' said Hando.
> '*You can have rice,*' replied his grandfather.
> *As he gazed at the meat hanging from the ceiling, Hando felt miserably hungry.*

Punctuating direct speech

This is simple direct speech:

> '*I wish I could have some of that pork,*' said Hando.

When you are punctuating it, remember to:

✔ open and close the speech marks

✔ add a comma before you close the speech marks

✔ start the 'said Hando' or 'he said' with a small letter

✔ put in a final full stop.

This is continued direct speech:

> '*I wish I could have some of that pork,*' said Hando sadly. '*But I know I can't.*'

When you are punctuating it, remember to:

✔ use a capital letter for the new sentence of direct speech in the second pair of speech marks

✔ put the final full stop inside the final speech mark.

A question mark or an exclamation mark can be used instead of a full stop:

> '*But I can't, can I?*'
> '*But I can't!*'

Writing out the story

◆ The paragraphs have been numbered for you.

◆ Indent them – start in from the margin with a clear capital letter.

◆ Set out the direct speech correctly.

◆ Punctuate the direct speech correctly.

◆ Write clearly – check your capital letters.

◆ Copy correctly – check your spelling of *successive; perhaps; stomach; ravenous; gnawing; preserved; uncomprehending.*

This is how your folk story could look. Check yours against it.

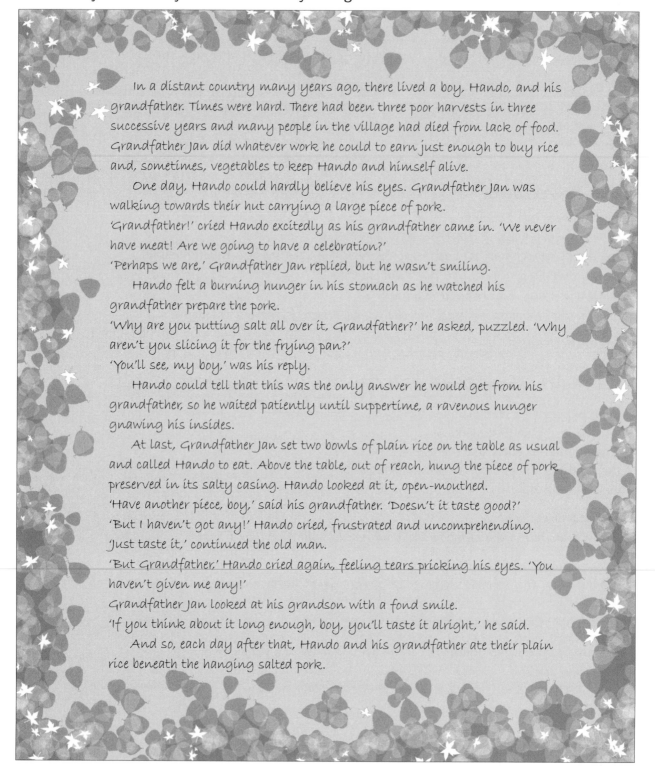

In a distant country many years ago, there lived a boy, Hando, and his grandfather. Times were hard. There had been three poor harvests in three successive years and many people in the village had died from lack of food. Grandfather Jan did whatever work he could to earn just enough to buy rice and, sometimes, vegetables to keep Hando and himself alive.

One day, Hando could hardly believe his eyes. Grandfather Jan was walking towards their hut carrying a large piece of pork.

'Grandfather!' cried Hando excitedly as his grandfather came in. 'We never have meat! Are we going to have a celebration?'

'Perhaps we are,' Grandfather Jan replied, but he wasn't smiling.

Hando felt a burning hunger in his stomach as he watched his grandfather prepare the pork.

'Why are you putting salt all over it, Grandfather?' he asked, puzzled. 'Why aren't you slicing it for the frying pan?'

'You'll see, my boy,' was his reply.

Hando could tell that this was the only answer he would get from his grandfather, so he waited patiently until suppertime, a ravenous hunger gnawing his insides.

At last, Grandfather Jan set two bowls of plain rice on the table as usual and called Hando to eat. Above the table, out of reach, hung the piece of pork preserved in its salty casing. Hando looked at it, open-mouthed.

'Have another piece, boy,' said his grandfather. 'Doesn't it taste good?'

'But I haven't got any!' Hando cried, frustrated and uncomprehending.

'Just taste it,' continued the old man.

'But Grandfather,' Hando cried again, feeling tears pricking his eyes. 'You haven't given me any!'

Grandfather Jan looked at his grandson with a fond smile.

'If you think about it long enough, boy, you'll taste it alright,' he said.

And so, each day after that, Hando and his grandfather ate their plain rice beneath the hanging salted pork.

Writing your own direct speech

❖ Write a conversation between two people on the topic of food.
❖ Write 12 lines.
❖ Set out and punctuate your direct speech correctly.
❖ Make the conversation as interesting as you can.

The Storm

At the beginning of the nineteenth century, Jane Austen visited the coastal town of Lyme Regis in Dorset. She found it so charming that she set some of the scenes in her novel *Persuasion* there. But life was not easy for the people who actually lived there. The price of bread had risen sharply and the poor were hungry.

Mary Anning was born into poverty at that time. Three children in her family had already died before she was born, but that still left eight others to be supported. Life was hard, so when news came of a touring company of entertainers visiting Lyme Regis, people were excited. There were to be displays of riding and competitions with prizes of unimaginable luxury, like legs of mutton.

Mary was just two years old when her nurse took her out to the field to watch the horse-riding stunts. The crowd was ecstatic and they hardly noticed when it started to rain, or even when thunder cracked. But then, suddenly, there was a flash of the most brilliant electric lightning ever seen followed by a deafening, shattering crash that echoed terrifyingly around the cliffs. Many in the crowd started to scream uncontrollably. With horror, they saw three women lying dead, including the nurse still clutching a limp and apparently lifeless Mary.

The child was carried back to her family's cottage by weeping neighbours. Her distraught mother took her in her arms and bathed her in hot water from the kettle. Gradually, Mary opened her eyes and, to the joy of the little crowd that had gathered, she revived completely. From that day on, she was much livelier and more intelligent than she had ever been before.

Nouns and adjectives

Nouns are words used for naming a person or thing.

◆ **Proper nouns** are the names of people, places, publications or events, and they take a capital letter: *Rufus; Australia; 'Great Expectations'; Christmas.* In this text: *Mary*

◆ **Concrete nouns** are names of things you can see and touch: *house; field; bath; dagger.* In this text: *nurse*

◆ **Abstract nouns** are names of things you cannot touch or see: *kindness; excitement; terror; intelligence.* In this text: *luxury*

Adjectives are words which qualify the noun. This means that they add to the meaning of the noun:

> ***enormous*** *tyres* = adjective + concrete noun
>
> ***enormous*** *wealth* = adjective + abstract noun

In this text:

> ***coastal*** *town* = adjective + concrete noun
>
> ***unimaginable*** *luxury* = adjective + abstract noun

The adjective doesn't always come before the noun. It can be placed elsewhere in the sentence:

> *The lottery winner's wealth was* ***enormous***.

Of course, there can be more than one adjective:

> *The lottery winner soon found that he had* ***new, demanding*** *'friends'.*

Adjectives can also be hyphenated:

> *The lottery winner's* ***long-standing*** *friends quickly disappeared.*

Adverbs

Adverbs are used to qualify any part of speech except a noun or pronoun. They are most often used to qualify verbs.

◆ They tell you more about the verbs
◆ They usually end in –ly, but not always: *cheerfully; fast*

> *The lottery winner* **quickly** *spent all his money on luxuries.*

Here, the adverb *quickly* qualifies the verb *spent* – it tells you **how** the winner spent his money.

In the text:

> *The price of bread had risen* **sharply**.

The adverb *sharply* qualifies the verb *had risen* – it tells you **how** the price had risen.

Personal pronouns

Personal pronouns are used to replace a noun or a noun phrase.

Personal pronouns are:

◆ singular personal pronouns: *I, you, she, he, it*
◆ plural personal pronouns: *we, they*

Take this sentence:

> *The little girl was fascinated by the hedgehog.*

The little girl is a noun phrase, and *hedgehog* is a noun.

The pronoun *she* can replace the noun phrase *the little girl*:

> *She was fascinated by the hedgehog.*

The pronoun *it* can replace the noun *hedgehog*:

> *The little girl was fascinated by it.*

In the text:

> *She found it so charming*

The pronoun *she* replaces the proper noun *Jane Austen*. The pronoun *it* replaces the noun phrase *the coastal town of Lyme Regis in Dorset*.

TASK

1 Make three columns headed:

   Proper nouns   Concrete nouns   Abstract nouns

   From the text, find as many examples as you can to write in your columns.

2 Make another three columns headed:

   Personal pronouns   Adjectives   Adverbs
   a) From the text, find examples of these parts of speech.
   b) Write down the part of speech and the word or words it qualifies.
   c) Write an explanation to identify the parts of speech, like this:

   Adjectives
   Weeping neighbours
   The adjective weeping qualifies the noun neighbours.

3 Write two paragraphs of your own in which you describe a dramatic incident.
   a) Use the six parts of speech you have been identifying.
   b) When you have finished, write a coloured key and colour code your six parts of speech.

This text comes from a leaflet which is published by FAUNA, an association which is trying to stop animal cruelty. In this text the way that chickens are taken for slaughter is described.

... A TALE OF SUFFERING AND MISERY

As if they haven't suffered enough, the infant birds still have to endure the nightmare of catching, transport and slaughter. This involves a gang of 'catchers', who seize the terrified birds by their feet, carrying as many as five birds at a time to a waiting lorry. With their frail legs and weak hearts they are fiercely stuffed and crammed into crates. Lids are violently slammed, with wings, legs or heads trapped. Rough handling results in broken bones. The operation is carried out at high speed with little or no regard for the welfare of the birds. Crates often get damaged and some birds fall from moving lorries and are killed on the roads. Transportation lorries are densely overcrowded. Over $2\frac{1}{2}$ million chickens die on the way to the slaughterhouse – victims of shock, stress, heat, cold, suffocation and injury. Chicken pieces on sale (legs and wings) will often have been removed from injured or diseased birds at the processing stage.

OVER 2 MILLION CHICKENS ARE BRUTALLY KILLED EVERY DAY IN BRITAIN

YOU CAN CHANGE THIS * DON'T BUY CHICKEN MEAT * JOIN US NOW!

LEARNING BOX

- The **literal meaning** of a word is its real meaning.
  For example, the literal meaning of 'chicken' is 'a young fowl,' or you could say, '*Literally, a chicken is a young fowl*'.
- An **abstract noun** is the name of a quality, something you cannot touch, e.g. terror, cruelty.
- An **adverb** tells you more about a **verb**. An adverb **qualifies** a verb and usually ends in *-ly*.
  For example, '*the chickens were cruelly treated*'.
- **Imperative verbs**, or verbs in the imperative mood, are in their command form. They give an order.
  For example, '*Join our club!*'; '*Help us to distribute leaflets!*'

EXAM TERMS

Explain When you are asked to explain something, you are being asked to make it clear. You could, for example, be asked to **explain** the meaning of a word, or how a writer has made the reader feel in a certain way.

Understanding and interpretation

1 What do the 'catchers' do?
2 Describe the birds' injuries in three sentences. Remember your full stops.
3 Why do chickens die on the way to the slaughterhouse?

Vocabulary

1 Look at the circled words *nightmare* and *gang*. What is the literal meaning of each word?
2 What do you associate with each word? Write down your answer in a list of abstract nouns, e.g. 'fear'.
3 How do these words help you to imagine how the chickens feel?
4 Look at the two underlined words *fiercely* and *violently*. They are adverbs. Write down these adverbs and the two verbs which they qualify. Label the words 'adverb' and 'verb'.
5 What kind of movement do the words describe?
6 What do the words tell you about the way the 'catchers' feel about the birds?
7 What other words in the text can you find which give a similar impression of the catchers?
8 The writer wants to persuade you to feel in a particular way. Look at the word *infant* in the first line. What is the literal meaning of 'infant'? Why does the writer use it to describe the young birds?
9 Find another word or phrase which makes you feel in a particular way, e.g. disgusted, sad. Explain how the words make you feel.

Evaluating the argument

1 Now that you have read this text, how do you feel about eating chicken?
2 How can you tell from the title that the writer is on the side of the chickens?
3 Summarize in three sentences the **purpose** of this text. Remember your full stops. For help with 'purpose', see the Exam Terms Box on page 61, in the 'Jungle Fever' task.

 ## TASK

You and some friends are writing a leaflet which is going to be distributed to students in your school. You are trying to persuade those people who read the leaflet to stop eating meat.

Use the text you have been working on in these pages to complete the following:

1 **Write an eye-catching heading for your leaflet**
    ◆ Make your heading a question, so that it involves your readers straight away.
    ◆ Remember to put a question mark at the end.
    ◆ You want to arouse strong feelings in your readers, so your question should make them feel strongly – for example, shocked, guilty or disgusted.
    ◆ Choose your words carefully to make your readers feel strongly. Use words with a strong emotional effect, such as *slaughter*; *murder*; *massacre*.

2   **Write out a *fact* from the text in capital letters**
    ◆ Choose a fact which you think will shock your readers.
    ◆ Underneath, write two questions directed to your readers which will make them feel guilty about eating meat now that they know the shocking fact you have told them.
    ◆ Don't forget your two question marks.

3   **Describe briefly and clearly one of the processes which happens to the animals**
    ◆ Use language which will horrify your readers.
    ◆ To describe the animals, use adjectives and nouns like *innocent* and *victims*, which make their treatment sound extremely cruel. Consider using the adjective *vulnerable*. Use a dictionary if necessary, and learn how to spell it.
    ◆ To describe the process and actions involved, use cruel, harsh verbs and adverbs, such as *thrust* and *roughly*.
    ◆ Tell the truth, and don't exaggerate.

4   **Write two bullet points at the end**
    ◆ Suggest what readers can do in each bullet point, such as '*Join our demonstration!*'
    ◆ Use imperative verbs (see the Learning Box).
    ◆ Make each bullet point brief and snappy.
    ◆ End each point with an exclamation mark.

Mark Honigsbaum is in the Venezuelan rainforests. He is with his trusted guide Hugo but, what with the rats, bugs, and vampire bats, he is having a terrible time. Hugo gets malaria and the only food is turtles from a lagoon …

Jungle Fever

The turtle soup was delicious, but that evening I could not shake off the nagging feeling that we had also brought another animal on board. I awoke full of energy but with a slight tingling in my foot. I slipped on my sandals and shuffled down to the river's edge where Hugo was already washing off the sweat of the previous night's fever.

'Marco, what is that boil on your toe?' I looked down. It was not a boil, exactly, but whatever it was it did not belong to me. Arturo came to investigate. 'Nigua', he said with a look of horror and unsheathed his machete. Hurriedly, I consulted my Brandt travel guide to Venezuela. 'Niguas are minute flesh-eaters, not to be confused with chiggers. They latch on if you walk bare-foot in contaminated places and set up home under the skin of the foot, usually at the side of a toenail where they lay a painful boil-like egg sac. These need picking out by a local expert …'

'Picking out, *not* amputation,' I enunciated.

'Marco, he does not understand. You will have to do it yourself. Don't you have anything small and sharp?'

But of course, the Swiss Army knife. As I now discovered, there really is a use for every attachment. In this case I was spoiled for choice: should I stab it with the corkscrew, impale it on the sharp chisel-like blade, or snip it with the scissors? I opted for the scissors. Several snips, and a lot of flayed skin later, the nigua was no more.

LEARNING BOX

- **Direct speech** records exactly what was said and puts it inside speech marks.
  For example: *'What is that boil on your toe?' asked Hugo.*
- **Reported speech** does not use the exact words, but reports what was said.
  For example: *Hugo asked what the boil on Marco's toe was.*

Direct speech is most commonly used in narrative writing. It has a more dramatic effect than reported speech. It also gives a greater sense of **immediacy**. This means it makes it seem as though it is actually happening as you read it.

- **Hyphenated adjectives**. A hyphen is the dash which links two words together to make one **hyphenated** word. Two examples of hyphenated adjectives are *rat-infested* and *sun-drenched*. They can be used to make descriptive writing more vivid. *We explored the rat-infested jungle* is a more dramatic and interesting way of saying *we explored the jungle, which was infested with rats*.

EXAM
TERMS

> **Purpose** You are often asked to explain **the writer's purpose**. This means you have to ask yourself '*Why* did the writer create this text?'
>
> To answer this question, you can explore reasons by asking yourself questions such as: 'Did he or she want to make me laugh?' 'Did he or she want to make me to share some pain?' 'Did he or she want to inform me?'

Before you start answering the questions:
◆ highlight the names of the three people in this text. They are Marco (the writer), Hugo (his guide) and Arturo (a Brazilian Indian).
◆ use a dictionary to find out the meanings of these words: *chiggers*; *machete*; *impale*; *flayed*

Understanding and interpretation
1 In the first paragraph, how does Marco know that something is not quite right with his toe?
2 How does Marco find out what a 'nigua' is? What information does he find out about it?
3 What is the treatment suggested for a *nigua* in the foot?
4 Why is Marco afraid of Arturo's machete?
5 How does Marco's Swiss Army knife come in handy?
6 How does he get rid of the *nigua*?

Vocabulary
1 Explain these words and phrases as they are used in the text: *the nagging feeling; investigate; unsheathed; latch on; contaminated; egg sac; amputation; spoiled for choice.*
2 Marco could make different kinds of attack on his toe with the various attachments on his Swiss Army knife. Which attachments can he choose from?
3 Explain the actions suggested by the words: *stab; impale; snip.*
4 What kind of movement is suggested by the word *shuffled* in the first paragraph? Why does Marco move in this way?
5 Look again at 'Direct speech' in the Learning Box.
   a) Highlight the direct speech in this text.
   b) Re-write all the direct speech as reported speech.
   Why do you think the writer chose to write this **direct speech**, rather than use **reported speech**?
6 In the second paragraph, in a different colour from the one you have already used, highlight the lines which are in quotation marks but which are not actually *spoken* by anyone. These lines are *not* direct speech. Why are they in quotation marks?

Purpose
Look again at the Exam Terms Box. Explain in **four** sentences the writer's purpose in 'Jungle Fever'.

Remember your four full stops.

TASK

Imagine you are Marco. You are in the rainforest with Hugo when you feel a crippling pain in your foot. A tiny but vicious spider has got inside your boot.

You need to write **three** paragraphs describing in a vivid and dramatic way what happens next. But before you start your writing, work through these exercises. You will then have plenty of ideas to help you.

1 Use some direct speech
- ◆ Check your punctuation by comparing it with the direct speech in the text.
- ◆ Use a new line for each speaker.
  For example:
  'Hugo! Help me! I've got red hot needles in my boot!' I cried.
  'What's up, Marco?' Hugo called out in a very worried voice.
  'Oh, God, there's something evil in my boot!' I answered, panic-stricken.
- ◆ Don't just write 'he said' or 'answered Hugo'. Liven your writing up as in the example above.
- ◆ Now write **four** lines of direct speech yourself.

2 Use vivid verbs and adjectives
Look back to the Learning Box. Remember that adjectives can be **hyphenated** to make them even more interesting. For example, instead of 'rainy' you could write 'rain-soaked'.

In the following clauses, change the dull **verb**, add an exciting **adjective** and finish the sentence in a dramatic and lively way. Underline your verb and adjective.
For example:
*When we **were** in the jungle, ...*
could be changed to:
*When we **were exploring** in the **insect-infested** jungle, I felt an agonizing jab inside my boot.*

Change and complete these clauses in the same way. Note the comma at the end of each clause. Make sure you include it.
*When I **went** into the hut , ...*
*After I **got** my sock off, ...*

Change the following dull **adjectives** into dramatic ones:
*The spider was **big**.*
Don't write *ginormous* or *humungous* because they are colloquial (slang) words – see the Learning Box for the 'Web of Deceit' task, page 64.
*The spider gave me a **really bad** bite.*
*The bite was **really painful**.*

3 Begin your mini-story in an interesting way
Think about writing a dramatic start for your story, which will immediately attract the attention of your readers.
Hugo and I were in the jungle when I got bitten by a spider.

This tells your readers where you were and what happened, but it's not **dramatic** or particularly **interesting**.

Think of films you have seen. They often start with a dramatic scene and some action. As soon as you see it, you are hooked. You want to watch the rest of the film. Try to do the same with your writing.
For example:
I was stumbling over tree roots. They were wet and slimy and felt like snakes twisting around my ankles. Suddenly, an agonizing pain shot through my foot.

Including a **simile**, in this case *like snakes*, adds to the **atmosphere** you are trying to create. Imagining the tree roots feeling like snakes in the jungle undergrowth adds to the feeling of horror and prepares the way for the spider bite. Include a simile in one of your opening sentences.

4   **Write your own mini-story**
    Now put together all your ideas and complete the writing of your story.

These are the headline, strap-line, picture caption and drop-in quote from an article in *The Guardian* by Jenny Madden. In it she tells how she was deceived by 'Simon', a man she met on an Internet dating site. She fell in love with him after they seemed to have so much in common. Much later she learned that he had hacked into her business and personal emails and that he was just playing games with her.

Headline

Web of deceit

Strap-line

Jenny Madden fell in love with a man she met on an internet dating site. It was only much later – after a romantic week together in Spain – that she realised the only reason they seemed to have so much in common was that he had been hacking into her email ...

Drop-in quote

This was the most powerful mental connection – I was in love with his mind

Look who's stalking ... Madden with some of the letters 'Simon' sent her before she realised that all was not what it seemed.

Picture caption

LEARNING BOX

- **Specialist vocabulary** includes words which are used in a particular field of interest. *Boot up, web site, chat room,* and *byte* are examples of the specialist vocabulary used for computers.
- A **pun** is a play on words, used usually for a lively or humorous effect. Puns are often used in newspaper headlines. For example, a report of a thief who was caught when a member of the public hit him in the face with a loaf of bread was headed *Breadly weapon*.
- The **literal** meaning of a word is its real meaning. For example, a *branch* is literally part of a tree. We use the word in a **metaphorical** sense and talk of a *branch of the family* or a *road branching off*.
- Words or expressions which are used in speech but not in formal writing are called **colloquial**. For example: *too much hassle; I've dumped him; ginormous*
- **Continuation dots** are the three dots used to show that a sentence is unfinished in some way. For example, *'You just wouldn't believe what he said then...'*

EXAM TERMS

Effect You are often asked to **analyse the effect** of a word or phrase. Writers choose to use the words they do, and write their sentences in the ways they do, because they want to make you, the reader, think and feel in a particular way. If, for example, they want to make you smile or laugh, they want their words to have a **humorous effect**. To **analyse** this effect, you would have to examine the words and explain how features such as their meanings, associations, significance, and sound help to make you feel or think in this particular way.

Understanding and interpretation

Headline

1 What is the **literal** meaning of the word *web*? That is, what is the *web* that you can see and touch?
2 What is the **metaphorical** meaning of the word *web*? That is, what can it mean when it is used metaphorically? Think of the expression in the sentence '*He was caught in a web of lies*'.
3 In the headline, there is **another** meaning to the word *web*, which is appropriate to an article about the Internet. What is it?
4 Why does *Web of Deceit* make a good headline?

Strap-line

1 What does the strap-line tell you about the article?
2 What effect does this have on the reader?
3 Why has the writer used the continuation dots?
4 Highlight the words which are connected with computers. What is the effect on the reader of this specialist vocabulary?
5 Why has the writer used the dashes around the phrase *after a romantic week together in Spain*?
6 Explain the contrast between the associations of *after a romantic week together in Spain* and *he had been hacking into her email*.
7 What does this contrast tell you about 'Simon', the man who deceived Jenny?

Picture caption

1 'Look who's talking' is a colloquial expression. How are the words *Look who's stalking* different from 'Look who's talking'?
2 Explain the different meanings of *talking* and *stalking*. Explain what the effect of this play on words is on the reader. Use the correct technical term from the Learning Box in your explanation.
3 Why is 'Simon' written in inverted commas?
4 Why does the writer include the continuation dots?

Drop-in quote

1 A drop-in quote is usually a sentence or phrase taken out of the main text. Where does a drop-in quote usually appear in a media article?
2 Why has this drop-in quote been chosen?
3 *Connection* has several meanings. Why is it a suitable word to describe the process of a woman falling in love with someone she has met on an Internet dating site?

TASK

All the features you have been discussing make this writing interesting. They catch your attention and arouse your curiosity. You want to know more. You want to read the article.

Using these to inspire you, write your own headline, strap-line, picture caption and drop-in quote for three articles on different topics:
1 a young woman who snatched a baby from a hospital maternity ward
2 an important football final
3 your own choice of topic.

This extract comes from Carlo Gebler's autobiography, *Father and I*. Here he recalls memories of his father and, in particular, a fishing trip with him on Lough Dan, a lake in Ireland. He was very young and was frightened when they caught a fish.

Father and I

I was a sickly infant, chesty, prone to wheezes. I remember the clang of spoon in cup as my father whipped my daily tonic of raw egg and a drop of sherry, the feel of the drinking cup on my lip, and finally, the alcohol and egg taste of the slippery, frothy, faintly mucus-like drink.

When I was one or a little older, my father took me out on Lough Dan in his boat. I remember holding the gunwale and peering at the smooth still black surface of the water. It began to rain gently. There was a smell of wet wool and brackish water and tar.

My father's rod swished in the air and the line paid out, whispering as it flew. The fly landed noiselessly on the surface. All was still and silent; then, suddenly, the rod whipped backwards and forwards and there was something silver in the water, twisting and turning as it rushed towards us. I whooped with excitement.

Then the silver form was in the boat. For a moment it lay on the boards. Then it arched and leapt into the air.

Terrified, I wailed.

'Be quiet,' said my father.

I was doubly frightened. Now, on top of the leaping silver terror, he was angry.

I began to cry.

'Didn't you hear me. Be quiet,' he shouted.

LEARNING BOX

- **The senses** are touch, taste, sight, hearing, and smell. The adjectives in the phrase *the sweet, red cherries* appeal to the senses of taste and sight.
- **Direct speech** records exactly what was said and puts it in speech marks. **Reported speech** does not use the exact words, but reports what was said.
  Direct speech: *'Please may I have some more?' asked Oliver.*
  Reported speech: *Oliver asked if he could have some more.*
- **Adjectives** describe or **qualify** the noun.
  In the *sweet, red cherries,* the words *sweet* and *red* are adjectives which qualify the noun *cherries.*
- You must **indent** each of your **paragraphs**. This means that you must start each first line of a paragraph about 3 centimetres in from the margin.

EXAM
TERMS

Conveys   When a writer **conveys** an atmosphere of, for example,
           suspense or terror, it means that he or she communicates those
           feelings to you, the reader. Through the choice of language, the
           writer gets those feelings across to you.

Analyse   When you are asked to **analyse** a writer's language, you have
           to break it down into parts, such as words, similes or direct
           speech, and comment on their significance and effect. You have
           to ask yourself questions such as 'What does that phrase
           suggest?', 'What does the sound of those words make me
           feel?', 'How does that simile add to the atmosphere?'

Understanding and interpretation

Look up these words in a dictionary:

mucus (noun)

gunwale (noun)

brackish (adjective)

Look at the first paragraph

1   What does Carlo's father give his little boy to drink each day?
2   Why does he give it him?
3   Explain how the writer's description appeals to the senses.

Read the rest of the text:

4   Describe in **four** clear sentences what happens in the text. Remember
    your full stops.
5   Re-write *'Be quiet,' said my father* as reported speech.
6   Highlight all the adjectives in the text in one colour and the nouns which
    they qualify in another colour.
7   Choose **three** adjectives and explain how they add to the vividness of the
    description.
8   Write down an example where the writer uses more than one adjective
    to qualify a noun.
9   Why do you think the writer does this?
10 Using words from the text, explain how the little boy's feelings change
    from excitement to fear.
11 Why is he suddenly frightened?
12 What kind of movement of the fish is suggested by the two verbs *arched*
    and *leapt*?
13 How does Carlo's father react to his little boy's fear?
14 Write down **three** different examples of descriptive words and phrases
    which appeal to the senses. How do you think they add to the 'feel' of
    the story?

TASK

In the story about Carlo and his father, the writer **conveys** atmosphere and
feelings vividly in a few words. You are also going to choose your words
carefully to **convey** atmosphere. (Look again at the Exam Terms Box for the
meaning of 'convey').

Think of an incident which takes place between a child and an adult. It could be something that happened to you or something you have read or heard about. It doesn't matter how small or unimportant the incident seems, because it is the *way* you write about it that is important.

Write a piece of continuous writing in two paragraphs describing the incident.

1   **Convey a vivid atmosphere**
    ◆ Use descriptive phrases which appeal to the senses, such as:
      The slapping of the water
    ◆ Use adjectives which appeal to the senses to describe your nouns, such as:
      *The **whispering** wind in the reeds*
    ◆ Use vivid verbs, not just dull ones like *got* or *went*:
      Does your character *go* inside, or does he *run, leap, dive, force his way, slip,* or *shuffle* inside?

2   **Write accurately**
    ◆ Use a full stop at the end of each sentence.
    ◆ Indent your paragraphs (see the Learning Box for 'indenting').
    ◆ Punctuate direct speech correctly and use a new line for each speaker.
    ◆ Use the apostrophe correctly:
      Carlo's father (possession); *I can't go* (omission).
    ◆ Use a connecting phrase followed by a comma to link your two paragraphs:
      All of a sudden, ...
      After a moment's silence, ...

3   **Analyse your writing**
    When you have finished, write a paragraph in which you **analyse** your own writing (see the Exam Terms Box for 'analyse').
    ◆ What atmosphere were you trying to convey?
    ◆ Why did you choose the words you did?
    ◆ Which part of your writing do you think was most successful? Why?
    ◆ Which part of your writing was the least successful? How could it have been improved?

FLYING: THE FACTS

Text A

Michael Gove describes how, after years of tranquil journeys, he has become crippled by fear as a result of one alarming experience

Flying with my wife-to-be to see relatives in France seemed relatively routine. Family and holiday visits, as well as cheap budget fares, had made the trip to Nice quite familiar, though still a treat. But that Friday in late August turned out quite differently from what I had come to expect. I first thought something might be wrong when I sensed that, though we had made good time, we seemed to have spent a surprisingly long period circling around Nice with the night lights of the Cote d'Azur twinkling below. Just as curiosity was shading into concern, the aircraft accelerated. Sharply.

The change in velocity and the rapid climb seemed to produce a G-force comparable with take-off. Children started crying, a few parents were shrieking. My wife tried to stand up and signal one of the attendants to find out what was going on. 'Why don't they tell us what's going on, people are panicking?' she asked. In front of us a husband who was trying to calm his own wife looked round sharply. 'Don't make a fuss,' he expostulated, as much in worry as anything. I tried to say calm. Inside my head, thoughts were racing. Was this some sort of engine fault, an evasive manoeuvre, the consequences of a cock-pit tussle between pilot and intruder or even a heart attack on the flight deck? Out of my mouth came, by contrast, what I hoped would be a soothing commentary for the benefit of myself as much as my wife and the couple in front. 'I'm sure everything is fine. If there's any sort of problem, we're within a short distance of the airport. It's the end of the flight so the fuel stocks will be lower and the risk of fire is less … Oh God, we're slowing down …'

And so we were. And levelling out. Then gently descending. The attendants looked relatively unruffled and said there had been 'some turbulence'. The pilot's voice came over the Tannoy telling us not to worry (don't they always say that, whatever is happening?), but no full explanation came. The descent, though smooth, was tense. Would fire engines meet us? In the end we landed perfectly. To loud applause.

Text B

Aviatours runs one of the largest courses for fear of flying. Five hundred people have taken a course since September 11, and 65 more will take one this week. They will learn that:

- An aircraft is kept aloft by the motion of air across the wings. The wings are shaped so that air travels more quickly over the top than over the bottom, thereby creating the required lift.
- An aircraft can glide for several minutes if the engines fail. A typical commercial plane can glide with no engine power, although it cannot land safely without power.
- Turbulence of the kind experienced in day-to-day flying is not dangerous. Aircraft have been tested to ensure that they can withstand it. Extreme turbulence can cause structural failure or loss of control, which is why all commercial aircraft are fitted with sophisticated weather radar systems, enabling the pilot to avoid the worst weather.
- Airclaims collate statistics on commercial flights around the world. They say that 66 commercial aircraft with 15 seats or more were lost in 2000, and there were 1,128 deaths. 1.91 billion people flew in that year. That is around one death for every 1.7 million flyers. Available figures for 2001 are 52 aircraft lost and 842 deaths.

LEARNING BOX

- Use a dictionary to explain the meanings of these words:
  tranquil (adjective)
  velocity (noun)
  G-force (noun)
  to expostulate (verb)
  to evade (verb)
  evasive (adjective)
  manoeuvre (noun)
  to applaud (verb)
  applause (noun)
  unruffled (adjective)
  turbulence (noun)

- A **question** has a question mark at the end and is addressed directly to the reader or someone in the text. A **statement** ends with a full stop. It reports a fact or an action, and does not address the reader directly.
  Question: *'Will we all die?'*
  Statement: *I wondered whether we would all die.*

- **Emotive language** is language which deliberately appeals to the emotions and stirs up strong feelings in the reader.
  For example: *rosy-cheeked infants; carnage in the park*

Understanding and interpretation

Text A

Paragraph 1

1. How has Michael felt about flying before that Friday in late August?
2. What first makes him think something might be wrong on the flight?
3. What really worries him?
4. What is the difference between feeling *curiosity* and feeling *concern*?
5. Give an example of a situation or happening which you might feel curious about, and one which you might feel concerned about. Explain your reasons.

Paragraph 2

1. How do the passengers in the plane behave after the aircraft accelerates?
2. Inside Michael's head are four ideas of what might be the cause of the acceleration. What are they?
3. He is frightened inside, but what does he actually say? Explain in reported speech. This means that you will start:

> Michael says that ...

4. Who is he helping by talking this way?

Paragraph 3

1. What happens after the plane starts slowing down?
2. How do the aircraft crew calm the passengers?
3. Why do the passengers applaud when the plane finally lands?

At the end of the first and third paragraphs, there is a very short sentence without a verb. Highlight both the sentences. Why has the writer used these short **verbless sentences**?

Use these words in your answer:
verbless sentences; emphasis (noun); *emphasize* (verb); *dramatic effect; emotion.*

There are several questions in this text. Highlight them. Why does the writer use questions, rather than statements? (See the Learning Box for 'question' and 'statement'.)

Use these words in your answer: *dramatic; personal; suspense; exciting.*

Text B

1   How many facts are given in each bullet point?
2   Explain how the shape of aircraft wings keeps a plane aloft.
3   Which fact would have comforted Michael?
4   What differences can you find in the way that Text A and Text B are presented? Look at features such as paragraphing; vocabulary; sentence structure; use of numbers.
5   What is the writer's purpose in this text?
6   What is Michael Gove's purpose in writing his account in Text A?

 TASK

A ride in your local amusement park went disastrously wrong last weekend. Several children were thrown out of a swinging chair and badly hurt.

1   Write two paragraphs from a newspaper report of this accident.
   ◆   Give your newspaper a name.
   ◆   Give your report a headline.
   ◆   Include date, place, facts of the accident.
   ◆   Use some dramatic language.
   ◆   Use some emotive language (see the Learning Box).
2   Write a letter to your local newspaper complaining about the dangers of the amusement park. See page 42 for the layout of a formal letter.
   ◆   Lay out your letter correctly.
   ◆   Write three paragraphs.
   ◆   Express your opinion forcefully.
   ◆   Be critical of the management of the amusement park.
   ◆   Use the weekend accident to strengthen your argument.

Extension for more able students

The section on pages 76–96 provides a variety of structured guidance designed to lift the performance of more able students so that they can achieve the highest possible grades. The units have all been carefully designed for students to work through on their own, or with minimal teacher help. The texts have been selected and the guidance has been written to target the higher level assessment objectives for both Reading and Writing in the specifications. But the students have not been burdened with 'AO-speak': the language in the guidance is accessible and clear.

WRITING UNITS

◆ A: Writing an article reviewing life so far
◆ B: Analysing in a written report the factors affecting post-GCSE students' decisions

These tasks offer guidance on answering two examination-style writing questions which were introduced in the *Student's Book*. The guidance assumes writing competence in the students and focuses on the acquisition of higher skills. For example, instruction is given not just on organizing material into paragraphs, but on arranging those paragraphs for a particular effect; on making an impact with titles, beginnings and conclusions; and on writing with flair and panache. Guidance is given on presenting objective analysis and in citing facts, figures, and evidence in an effective way.

READING TO WRITE UNIT: TEACHER-FREE!

Murder in the Mist

For this **fully photocopiable** unit (PCMs 19–21), a thought-provoking report on the killing of mountain gorillas has been written specifically to illustrate particular features of high quality writing. Students can work through it entirely on their own at home or in school, or as a group.

The structured guidance which follows the text focuses on areas of the writing for students to analyse, and finally to use in their own writing of a report on a different topic. The areas covered include achieving the economy of vigorous writing through choice of vocabulary; appreciating the complexity and subtlety of verb tenses and forms; and expressing a viewpoint powerfully through understatement.

READING UNITS

The texts offered here are from a variety of printed sources including newspaper articles, opinion pieces, and memoir. They have been selected to stimulate and challenge students, and some have been paired to enable students to make insightful and probing cross references. The opinion pieces are trenchant and students will be able to extend their vocabularies by internalizing the writers' use of language. They should prompt lively discussion, and be read with pleasure.

To focus students on their choice of language and sentence structure, and to encourage them to write succinctly and effectively, they are asked to write only paragraphs, not complete essays. These could, of course, be 'worked up' into complete assignments and used for non-fiction coursework.

- A: *The Anoraks* – a strong opinion piece which argues that 'anoraks' such as train-spotters and amateurs with metal detectors should be admired. Students are advised how to embed apt and pithy quotation; to interpret meaning and extend their vocabularies; and to appreciate the function of illustration. Their tasks focus on expressing opinion and on analysing their own work.

- B: *The Most Magical Grandmother* and *Time is Short* – Prince Charles's emotional and personal tribute to his grandmother, the Queen Mother, contrasts sharply with the view given in the other text that she was one who 'endorsed luxury and idleness'. Students evaluate how opinion and fact are presented; extend their word power; and make detailed cross references. The tasks require students to write in different formats, from various contrasting viewpoints.

- C: *I'm Like a Bird* – Nick Hornby's opinion piece on pop music in general, and Nelly Furtado's single 'I'm Like a Bird' in particular. Students are questioned on the interpretation of the writer's words and guided through an analysis and evaluation of the range of language and sentence structure. Students are asked to write provocatively on a controversial topic, changing their tone half-way through.

- D: *The Habit* and *rush hour* – a writer remembers himself as a child 'reading catatonically', and an extract from a travel company brochure challenges the reader to sign up for 'full-on fun and excitement'. Students compare the audiences and the language of these two contrasting texts; they are asked to write for two different audiences and to include specific features in their texts.

Task from the *Students' Book*, page 93

Write an article for a magazine in which you review your life so far. Focus on the lessons for life which you feel you have learned over the years.

What you *don't* want to do in answering this question is merely to relate anecdotes about your life. The focus of your article should be on the lessons for life which you have learned. The overall mood will be reflective.

Organization

Making a list like the one below will help you decide on what these life lessons are. Mature students will have had wider experience of life and perhaps a longer list of lessons learned!

What happened in my life	What life lesson I learned
I've had to work really hard for my exams	discipline; self motivation
I was bullied for a year when I was 9	self-control; to hide my emotions
My parents' marriage broke up	not to trust people easily; self-reliance; cynicism
My best friend and I have been friends for 11 years	the value of faithfulness and friendship
My Gran died	to understand and accept death
I have helped to look after my half-sister since she was born 2 years ago	giving and receiving love is the best thing in the world
I have a Saturday job	to be reliable; to be polite to people even if I don't like them
I have had my dog for the last 10 years	animals are often more faithful than human beings

When you have collected all your ideas together, plan four or five paragraphs each dealing with a theme.

Next, think about how to arrange those paragraphs, so that there is some purpose in the arrangement. You could, for example, have a contrast between them: optimism could be followed by cynicism, or friendship followed by loss of trust. Variations in language, sentence structure and tone as well as theme will also make your paragraphs contrast effectively.

Another effective arrangement could be chronological, starting with the lessons you learned as a very young child.

Whichever arrangement you choose, think of effective phrases or sentences to link the paragraphs together.

Starting and ending with a bang, not a whimper

◆ **Make an impact with the title you give your article.**
My Life or *What My Life has Taught Me* would be appropriate, but not **punchy**. You want a title that will arrest the reader's attention by being intriguing or amusing. Play around with ideas using puns, questions, quotations, proverbs, colloquialisms, and alliteration to come up with something more arresting:

> Older and Wiser?
> A Bed of Roses – Not!
> 'Full of Sound and Fury'?

◆ **Make an impact with your first few sentences.**
Try directing a question with emotion, drama, humour, irony, or (as below) cynicism at the reader.

> Do you remember those days when life was tinged with a rosy glow?
> When it was always summer and there were no exams? Excuse me
> while I take off my rose-coloured spectacles!

Experiment with your own ideas and introductory sentences. Produce sentences which shake the reader awake, as in the example above.

◆ **Make an impact with your conclusion.**
You don't want to end on a dull note. Experiment with:
✔ an element of controlled humour
✔ a witty or thoughtful reference back to your title
✔ a question directed to your reader
✔ a reflective concluding comment
✔ an emotional and moving comment.

> Older and Wiser?
> I'm definitely older than I was when I was born. But how much wiser am I?
> Sometimes I think I've learned all there is to know, but then the exams come
> along, and I think I know nothing at all!
>
> A Bed of Roses – Not!
> Sometimes I wish that I could return to those days of childhood when my
> family was happy and the sun was always shining. But a life lesson I have
> learned, the one which is the hardest to accept, is that you can't go back.

Writing with flair

Flair, style, panache – this is what makes writing fly.

Some writers can write brilliantly without any effort. Most have to work at it!

Consider the following extract:

> I love my baby sister. She is fourteen years younger than me and I suppose I am a second mother to her. I have learned so much from looking after her and seeing her grow. Most of all I have learned that you can't do anything more worthwhile in life than give and receive love.

✔ entirely appropriate and focused
✔ accurate
✔ expressed in moving terms

What is lacking is *flair* and *panache*.

Try painting a vignette or scenario to create the atmosphere you want, and then make your reflective comment:

> Wisps of gold hair encircling a tiny, perfect sleeping face: this was my first sighting of my baby sister two years ago. Since that time, I have been a second mother to her and she has often been less than perfect! But what feeling in the world can compare with her arms wound tightly round my neck and her smile that always lightens even my darkest moods? From her I have learned the greatest life lesson of all. The priceless value of love.

✔ arresting and intriguing opening sentence
✔ powerful emotional and visual appeal combined in initial image
✔ emotional force conveyed through the choice of vocabulary
✔ a touch of humour to lighten mood
✔ focuses on the question, and the 'review' element is clear
✔ avoids cliché and sentimentality
✔ variation of sentence structure (colon; exclamation; question; brief sentence for effect)
✔ vocabulary sensitively chosen
✔ sentence begun with a connective for effect
✔ qualifiers add interest and atmosphere
✔ variation of verb forms
✔ final verbless sentence used for effect.

PCM
17

BRAINSTORMING

'Lessons for life' review

What happened in my life	What lesson I learned
1	1
2	2
3	3

Ideas for title

Ideas for opening sentences

Ideas for conclusion

Ideas for adding flair to my writing

Task from the *Students' Book,* page 90

A programme researcher is asking young people to help him with his planning for a television series. Write a report for the researcher in which you analyse the factors which you think affect students' decisions as to whether or not to stay on in education after GCSEs.

Organization

Discussing the topic with a group is a good way of collecting ideas for your report. Whichever way you prepare for the task, writing a list of factors with brief notes will help you marshal the points you are going to make.

Factors affecting students' decision to stay on in education after GCSEs

Money

Wanting the independence that a job and money brings

Wanting things like a car, computer equipment now

What a 16-year-old's wages buy in reality

Difficulties of low-income families supporting post-16 children in education

Family support

Parents may encourage or even insist on further education

Parents may discourage or even forbid further education

Experiences of brothers and sisters will influence students' decisions

Work

Getting a job seems attractive because of gaining independence

But low wages/insecure job market cause problems

Difference between opportunities for girls and boys of 16 in job market

Career opportunities and wages will be greater with qualifications

Experience of school

Social and educational experiences at school will affect the decision to stay on

Successful students will want to go on; unhappy, unsuccessful students won't

Teachers can be an encouragement or, if students don't like them, a discouragement.

You have your heading for the report here:

> Factors affecting students' decision to stay on in education after GCSEs

You could divide your report under three subheadings:

> Money and Work
> Experience of School
> Family Support

Underneath each heading write your *indented* paragraphs.

Your report is for a television researcher, who would doubtless appreciate personal, humorous touches in your writing which will bring it alive. It is a report about people, after all. Most important, however, is the *analysis of the factors*. It isn't a matter of being right or wrong, because *your* opinion, experience, and observations will be the basis for your analysis.

Objective analysis

On the topic of 'Money and work', you might say:

> It is attractive to 16-year-olds to get a job and earn money to buy all the material possessions which they can't afford whilst studying at school. A dream car and designer clothes could be theirs!

To extend this statement into objective analysis, you need to examine the key issues which your statement has raised, such as: What kind of money will a 16-year-old earn? What kind of work would be available? Is this dream realistic? You could continue:

> However, looking at it more realistically, this idealistic vision of freedom and big-spending independence isn't quite what it seems. Those 16-year-olds who can see further than the immediate future see something different. The money might look good now whilst living at home with Mum buying your food, but what about £4 or £5 an hour when you're 30 years old? Not so good! These more far-sighted 16-year-olds would rather stay on for further education and be earning perhaps £30,000 a year by the time they're 30.
>
> Looked at more closely, though, the choice is not so simple because other factors are involved. Perhaps the 16-year-old choosing work rather than education has social reasons, such as a low-income family, for doing so. Many parents cannot afford to support a son or daughter ...

This kind of analytical writing shows a range of commendable qualities:
- ✔ Analytical markers such as *However, looking at it more realistically* and *Looked at more closely* show control. Use some similar markers yourself.
- ✔ The analysis is objective: judgements are not made explicitly, but different aspects of the issue – idealistic, realistic, and career expectations – are raised and considered.
- ✔ The complexity of the issues raised is appreciated.
- ✔ Details of earnings give authenticity and interest.
- ✔ The reference to *Mum buying your food* lightens the tone, without diminishing the serious point.
- ✔ Varied sentence structure is used for effect, e.g. question; verbless exclamation.

Citing facts, figures, and evidence

Analysis is often more convincing if it is supported by objective facts or valid statistics. If, for example, you were reading an article about the poverty of families in rural England, it would be more effective if the writer gave you the accurate income levels of those families. You might not be able to produce facts and figures about students' decisions to stay on in education, but you could bring in something that you have read in the newspaper or heard on the television to expand your analysis.

> The government is proposing a wonderful new scheme. It has come up with the clever idea of _paying_ students £40 a week to stay on at school! This will make everyone stay on and achieve great things, they say. Has the government not thought about students keeping the £40 and just turning up for the odd lesson? Spending it on CDs and clothes instead of bus fares and books? Seriously, though, paying students to take up further education might motivate them to sign up, but not to do the work.

✔ Uses evidence from the media/current affairs to extend analysis.
✔ Challenges and analyses this evidence.
✔ Without explicit condemnation, expresses opinion and judgement through subtle irony, e.g. _wonderful new scheme, clever idea_, and through the exclamation mark and underlining.
✔ A well-judged colloquialism adds impact to the ironic tone: _turning up for the odd lesson_.
✔ Variation in sentence structure: questions, exclamation, well-balanced clauses.

Concluding your report

◆ Write a concluding sentence which brings the threads of your report together.
◆ Sign off your report with your name, and information which you judge would be useful for the researcher, such as your age, address, and school.

PCM
18

BRAINSTORMING
– a report on students' decisions about education

Factors affecting their decision	Points for objective analysis
Money and work	
1	1
2	2
3	3
4	4
	Facts, figures, and evidence to use
Experience of school	
1	1
2	2
3	3
4	4
	Ideas for concluding sentence
Family support	
1	
2	
3	
4	

Murder in the Mist

Tourists in Rwanda pay £200 to spend an hour observing endangered mountain gorillas in their natural habitat. This lucrative tourist industry creates a dilemma for conservationists: the gorillas become accustomed to human contact and this increases their vulnerability. Yet without the financial resources earned by tourism, the extinction of the last 350 pairs of these rare creatures in Rwanda is inevitable.

Now the callous cruelty of selfish individuals has brought the gorillas' death knell a little closer. Two adult female gorillas have been killed and an adult male shot and wounded as they fought in vain to defend their family group. A three-year-old gorilla is missing and a one-year-old which had escaped capture was found desperately trying to suckle from its dead mother a day after the attack. Fourteen national park employees have been arrested.

'Mountain gorillas are truly precious,' says the National Parks Director in Rwanda. 'Imagine how much money a collector would pay to own one. Many millions of dollars. Only someone in the West has that kind of money. Whoever perpetrated this crime undoubtedly did so on the orders of a dealer who was acting on behalf of a wealthy Western client.'

So where will that young gorilla end up? In a private collection of some obscenely rich Westerner?

'Probably not, although that would have been the intention,' says the Director. 'No mountain gorilla has ever survived in captivity. That priceless young animal is almost certainly dead.'

It is both tragic and ironic that this savage blow to the gorillas should have been dealt by employees of the National Parks. It had seemed that at last the Rwandans had learned to regard the gorillas as a source of national pride, rather than as animals to be hunted for meat. But some locals, clearly, could not resist the lure of a Westerner's promise of unimaginable wealth. This is no surprise in a poor country, but how immeasurably sad it is that the Westerner with millions of dollars to spare sought to satisfy only his overweening selfishness, and not to benefit the world by making a real contribution to the survival of the animals he obviously prizes.

Report by Jess Hart, Rwanda

The title

Titles are there to attract the reader. This one certainly does.

In it, there is an allusion to the film *Gorillas in the Mist*. The film showed the valuable work with these gorillas done by the primatologist, Dr Dian Fossey.

- How effective do you think this title is?
- Suggest two alternative titles for this report.

Economy

Writing at length is not a virtue. Writing with succinctness and economy is!

- Aim to be precise and concise in your choice of language. In the first paragraph, the single noun *dilemma* is more sophisticated, accurate and vigorous than the equivalent noun phrase *difficult problem*.
- Find four other examples of vocabulary which you think contributes to the precision and effectiveness of this text.
- Explain the effectiveness of your examples.

Verbs

Analyse the variety of verb forms and tenses which are used in the text. Find examples of the following:

- present tense
- different forms of past tense
- imperative
- future
- conditional
- passive

What do you think this variety of verb forms brings to the text?

Direct speech

Direct speech breaks up continuous prose and adds interest.

In the Director's direct speech:

- What do the phrases *truly precious* and *that priceless young animal* tell you about his feelings for the gorillas?
- What does the clause *Whoever perpetrated this crime* tell you about his tone?
- What do you learn about his view of the West?

Asking questions

Linking the two pieces of the Director's direct speech is this:

> *So where will that young gorilla end up? In a private collection of some obscenely rich Westerner?*

The writer could have written these questions in reported speech.

> *I then asked the Director where the young gorilla would end up. I suggested it might end up in a private collection of some obscenely rich Westerner.*

Alternatively, she could have put her questions into direct speech:

> *'Where will that young gorilla end up?' I asked the Director. 'In a private collection of some obscenely rich Westerner?'*

- Consider the effectiveness of each of these methods.
- Which do you think is the most successful? Explain your reasons.

Viewpoint

Subtlety and understatement are usually far more effective than over-writing.

Consider:

A one-year-old which had escaped capture was found desperately trying to suckle from its dead mother.

The author could have written:

A one-year-old which had escaped capture was found desperately trying to suckle from the blood-soaked dugs of its murdered mother.

◆ Analyse the different effects of the two sentences.
◆ Consider how effectively each conveys the writer's viewpoint.
◆ Which do you think is most effective and why?
◆ Analyse the viewpoints expressed elsewhere in the text.

Variety of sentence structure

Sometimes a simple sentence is both appropriate and effective:

Fourteen national park employees have been arrested.

Simple sentences are effective when they make a contrast with other, complex sentences. A complex sentence must be controlled to be effective.

Consider this complex sentence:

This is no surprise in a poor country, but how immeasurably sad it is that the Westerner with millions of dollars to spare sought to satisfy only his overweening selfishness, and not to benefit the world by making a real contribution to the survival of the animals he obviously prizes.

◆ Break down this sentence into clauses.
◆ Identify the verbs.
◆ Identify the connectives and analyse their function.
◆ *How immeasurably sad it is* could have been written *it is immeasurably sad*. Analyse the comparative effectiveness of the two structures.

 TASK

Write a report on an item in the news in this country or abroad.
◆ Inform the reader of the events or situation.
◆ Give essential background information.
◆ Include some direct speech.
◆ Convey different viewpoints.
◆ Convey your own viewpoint.
◆ Maintain an appropriate tone.
◆ Use language concisely and powerfully.
◆ Use a variety of sentence structures.

In April 2002, Cliff Bradshaw, an amateur with a metal detector, unearthed a spectacular Bronze Age gold cup worth £250,000. In this extract from his article, Roy Hattersley argues that his discovery is a vindication for all those people who are accused of wasting their time on hopeless projects.

Roy Hattersley

'The anoraks deserve the praise of everyone who despises the half-hearted'

Had the Wright brothers not made their aeroplane fly they would have remained no more than owners of a bicycle factory in Dayton, Ohio, who had a crazy notion about men possessing the power of birds. And if Edward Jenner had not developed the vaccine which eliminated smallpox he would be remembered (if at all) as the pathetic doctor who wasted his life – and caused a good deal of human suffering – in pursuit of a formula which all his medical contemporaries knew could not be found.

For every successful Wright and Jenner there have to be thousands of failed engineers and physicians. Without the multitudes of men and women whose metal detectors tick in vain, Cliff Bradshaw would not have found what looks like a replica of the Holy Grail. The Holy Grail is the perfect example of the pointless obsession which, by some quirk of human psychology, attracts nothing but credit to those it dominates. Joseph of Arimathea did not bring to England the cup from which Christ drank at the Last Supper. Yet King Arthur and his Knights of the Round Table spent most of their lives looking for it in and around Camelot. Sir Galahad searched with the manic determination of a stamp collector who has mislaid his 'penny black'. Nobody called him a nerd. It all goes to prove that times, and values, change. In an age of diminished attention spans – when some of our children can only concentrate for as long as it takes to change a television channel – we crudely undervalue the men and women who devote all their time and enthusiasm to the pursuit of a single infatuation. The train-spotters, the stamp collectors and the football statisticians who cannot only remember who won the Cup in 1935 but can name both teams which played in the Final and the players who scored the goals are dismissed as 'anoraks' and described by the 21st century's two most damning adjectives – sad and boring. We ought to admire their persistence, their devotion and indomitable determination. They are true 'amateurs' – men and women motivated purely by love.

How to quote effectively

Look at the following question, and the beginning of the student's answer:

Explain Hattersley's final conclusion about people who devote themselves to pursuing a single infatuation like train-spotting. Quote from the text to support your answer.

Hattersley thinks that we should admire these people. He says: 'We ought to admire their persistence, their devotion and indomitable determination'. He admires them because they are driven by love. He says: 'They are true "amateurs" – men and women motivated purely by love.'

Assessment comments
✔ Hattersley's conclusion is made clear.
✔ There is appropriate selection from the text.
✗ The paragraph relies on writing out Hattersley's words.
✗ It is repetitive rather than interpretative.

A better way

There is a much more effective and sophisticated way to quote. Select **brief**, **apt** words and phrases and **embed** them into your own prose (embedding a quotation means putting it within your sentences, not copying out separate lines). Instead of just *repeating* what your quotation says, *interpret* it:

In his conclusion, Hattersley expresses his admiration for the dogged hard work of these enthusiasts. He sees their 'persistence, their devotion and indomitable determination' as impressive and not as something to be mocked. His final words are praise for the sincerity of those enthusiasts 'motivated purely by love' who are amateurs in the true sense of the word.

Assessment comments
✔ Hattersley's conclusion is clearly and economically explained.
✔ There is appropriate and brief quotation from the text.
✔ Quotations are effectively embedded.
✔ The writer's words are interpreted.

Understanding and interpretation

Answer the following questions, quoting from the text to support your answers.
1 How are the pursuits of the metal detector Cliff Bradshaw and King Arthur and his Knights similar?
2 Why does Hattersley use King Arthur and his Knights as an example?
3 What criticisms does Hattersley make about today's society and its attitudes?

Vocabulary

1 Analyse the effect of these words in the second paragraph:
   ◆ *nerd*
   ◆ *anoraks*

2 Explain concisely the meanings of these phrases:
   ◆ *by some quirk of human psychology*
   ◆ *the pursuit of a single infatuation*
   ◆ *men and women motivated purely by love*

3 Explain the meanings of these words as they are used in the text:
   ◆ *quirk*
   ◆ *indomitable*
   ◆ *notion*
   ◆ *diminished*

4 Take the topic 'War is Never Justified'. Write **four** sentences, either separate or linked in continuous prose. Make a powerful and persuasive point in each sentence using the words in Questions 2 and 3 above.

Analysis of the effect of sentence structure

Identify and analyse the effect of the following in the first paragraph:
◆ verb tenses and forms
◆ starting a sentence with a connective
◆ parenthetical brackets
◆ parenthetical dashes
◆ structure of a complex sentence.

In the second paragraph, analyse the effect of:
◆ the short sentence.

Illustration in support of the argument

Explain briefly who or what were:
◆ the Wright brothers
◆ Edward Jenner
◆ Joseph of Arimathea
◆ Sir Galahad
◆ the penny black

What is the function of illustration in an argument? Analyse the effectiveness of each of these particular illustrations in Hattersley's argument.

 TASK

1 Using what you have learned from analysing the text, write a paragraph in which you present a single strand of argument on the topic 'War is Never Justified'. You can, of course, argue for or against the topic.

   In your paragraph use:
   ◆ a question for effect
   ◆ a brief sentence for effect
   ◆ at least one powerful and persuasive illustration
   ◆ some sophisticated vocabulary.

2 Underneath, write an analysis of your own paragraph. Explain:
   ◆ the effects you wanted to achieve
   ◆ how you tried to achieve these effects
   ◆ how successful you think you were.

These two media extracts are about the death of the Queen Mother in April 2002. The first one is from *The Daily Telegraph* and reports Prince Charles' emotional response to his grandmother's death. The second one is from an opinion article in *The Guardian* in which the writer expresses a very different response to the Queen Mother's death.

Text A

'The most magical grandmother'

By Caroline Davies

The Prince of Wales yesterday paid an emotional and highly personal tribute to Queen Elizabeth the Queen Mother.

'She was quite simply the most magical grandmother you could possibly have and I was utterly devoted to her,' he said.

At times close to tears, he spoke of her as 'irreplaceable'. She had left a chasm.

'For me, she meant everything and I had dreaded, dreaded this moment. Somehow I never thought it would come. She seemed gloriously unstoppable.'

The Queen Mother had become 'an institution in her own right', he said.

Wearing a dark suit and black tie, the Prince gave the five-minute televised address in the Orchard Room at Highgrove, his Gloucestershire home. Behind him on a table was a silver-framed portrait of the Queen Mother standing on the steps of her Scottish retreat, the Castle of Mey.

Next to it was another portrait of her smiling in a blue feathered hat and pearl necklace. At the bottom was written in faded black ink: 'With much love, Granny. 1976.'

> **'an institution in her own right'**

Prince Charles, whose relationship with the Queen Mother was particularly close, spoke of her great emotional legacy.

Glancing occasionally at the brief hand-written notes on his lap, he described her as 'at once indomitable, somehow timeless, able to span the generations; wise, loving, and an utterly irresistible mischievousness of spirit'.

He said: 'Above all, she understood the British character and her heart belonged to this ancient land and its equally indomitable and humorous inhabitants, whom she served with panache, style and unswerving dignity for very nearly 80 years.'

Struggling with his emotions, he added: 'Oh, how I shall miss her laugh.'

He paid his tribute as the Queen and senior members of the Royal Family spent the day at Windsor Castle coming to terms with the Queen Mother's death on Saturday.

Text B

Time is short for the elderly Queen, her arrogant consort and self-pitying son

The breeding of a 'master family' is not much different in principle from the breeding of a master race; it involves much the same combination of the ridiculous and the sinister, and is every bit as incompatible with democracy and civilisation. It will not be recorded by history that the Queen Mother's progeny were exceptional except in their egotism and pettiness: not even her stoic and dutiful eldest daughter can escape some part of the blame.

The flags that now dip are also standards that have fallen. Much of the emotion of the leavetaking will be genuine (in spite of the yellow-press effort to make it seem bogus by hysterical over-statement). It will be genuine because it is a tribute to longevity confused with a tribute to history. And it will also be genuine because it is a farewell to something that is irretrievably lost – the authority of monarchy in Britain. We are left alone with our day, and the time is short for the elderly Queen and for her arrogant consort and self-pitying son. Republicans should still be modest, because this is not yet their triumph. It was the hereditary concept itself which produced a woman who symbolised and endorsed luxury and idleness in personal life, philistinism in culture, ruthlessness in eugenics and reaction in politics. The mourning will necessarily be brief: no serious people can truly regret the passing of an epoch such as that.

Christopher Hitchens

Interpreting fact and opinion

1 What made the Queen Mother 'a magical grandmother' to Prince Charles?
2 How can you tell that Prince Charles' tribute to his grandmother is 'highly personal'?
3 How does Christopher Hitchens feel about the death of the Queen Mother?
4 What does he believe the Queen Mother symbolized?
5 Explain the opinion expressed in the first paragraph.

Vocabulary

Text A

1 Explain the meanings of: *indomitable; panache*
2 Explain Prince Charles's incorrect use of the word *humorous*. What does the error tell you about the tribute?

Text B

1 Explain the meanings of these words as they are used in the text:
   progeny; egotism; pettiness; stoic; bogus; hysterical; longevity; endorsed; epoch.
2 Explain the meanings of these phrases as they are used in the text:
   incompatible with democracy and civilisation; the hereditary concept; philistinism in culture; ruthlessness in eugenics; reaction in politics.

Evaluating how opinion is presented

Text A

Most of Text A quotes Prince Charles's exact words, but there are some linking sentences written by the reporter. Highlight these linking sentences and consider:

1 What effect does the reporter want to achieve by including the detailed descriptions of the framed photographs?
2 What effect do the writer's phrases *struggling with his emotions* and *coming to terms with* have?
3 In Prince Charles's tribute, what is the effect of the repetition in *'I had dreaded, dreaded this moment'*?
4 What is the effect of the word *Oh* and the phrase *how I shall* in *'Oh, how I shall miss her laugh'*?

Text B

1 The writer is critical of the monarchy as an institution, individual members of the royal family, and the popular press *(the yellow press)*. Explain these criticisms briefly and analyse the effect of the words chosen by the writer to express them.
2 How does the writer's use of adjectives and abstract nouns help to convey the forcefulness of his opinion?
3 Highlight the verbs. How do they contribute to the writer's assertive tone?
4 Take Christopher Hitchens's argument. Write four of your own sentences in which you seek to *persuade* your readers of the same argument. Use persuasive verb forms and persuasive phrases.

Making cross references

1 How do the writers' aims in the two texts differ?
2 How does the tone of the two texts differ?
3 Compare the effects of the language and the sentence structure in the two texts.
4 Compare the likely reactions of readers to the two texts.

⋀⋀ TASK

1 There has been a train derailment in Northumberland, in which 26 people have been killed and many more injured. The cause was a rail which had been reported as faulty, but which had not been mended. Write the introductory paragraphs to two separate media pieces:
   a) an emotional 'on-the-spot' account of the rescue
   b) a harsh criticism of the rail authorities.
2 Write two letters to the Editor of *The Guardian* in which you express views on Christopher Hitchens's opinions. For layout of a formal letter, see page 42.
   a) Write the first letter as though you were a loyal royalist (someone who loves the royal family and is in favour of the monarchy).
   b) Write the second letter as though you were a staunch republican (someone who is strongly in favour of getting rid of the hereditary monarchy).

Nick Hornby says he has been driven 'potty with pleasure' by Nelly Furtado's single 'I'm Like a Bird'. Here are the opening three paragraphs of his opinion piece about that song, and pop music in general.

Nick Hornby wrote the novels *High Fidelity, Fever Pitch,* and *About a Boy,* all of which have been made into highly successful films.

I'm Like a Bird

Of course I can understand people dismissing pop music. I know that a lot of it, nearly all of it, is trashy, unimaginative, poorly written, slickly produced, inane, repetitive and juvenile (although at least four of these adjectives could be used to describe the incessant attacks on pop that you can still find in posh magazines and newspapers); I know too, believe me, that Cole Porter was 'better' than Madonna or Travis, that most pop songs are aimed cynically at a target audience three decades younger than I am, that in any case the golden age was thirty-five years ago and there has been very little of value since. It's just that there's this song I heard on the radio, and I bought the CD, and now I have to hear it ten or fifteen times a day …

That's the thing that puzzles me about those of you who feel that contemporary pop (and I use the word to encompass soul, reggae, country, rock – anything and everything that you might regard as trash) is beneath you, or behind you, or beyond you – some preposition denoting distance, anyway: does this mean that you never hear, or at least never enjoy, new songs, that everything you sing in the shower was written years, decades, centuries ago? Do you really deny yourselves the pleasure of mastering a new tune (a pleasure, incidentally, that your kind is perhaps the first in history to forgo) because you are afraid it might make you look as if you don't know who Foucault is? I'll bet you're fun at parties.

See, the song that has been driving me potty with pleasure recently is 'I'm Like a Bird', by Nelly Furtado. Only history will judge whether Ms Furtado turns out to be any kind of artist, and though I have my suspicions that she will not change the way we look at the world, I can't say that I'm very bothered: I will always be grateful to her for creating in me the narcotic need to hear her song again and again. It is, after all, a harmless need, easily satisfied, and there are few enough of those in the world. I don't even want to make a case for this song, as opposed to any other – although I happen to think that it's a very good pop song, with a dreamy languor and a bruised optimism that immediately distinguishes it from its anaemic and stunted peers. The point is that a few months ago it didn't exist, at least as far as we are concerned, and now here it is, and that, in itself, is a small miracle.

Nick Hornby

Understanding and interpretation

1   Explain succinctly Hornby's argument in each of the three paragraphs.
2   To whom is the text addressed?
3   Explore how the tone in which Hornby addresses his audience changes between the first and second paragraphs.

4   What does the adjective *posh* tell you about Hornby's view of the magazines and newspapers which attack pop music?
5   What does the adverb *cynically* tell you about Hornby's view of today's record producers?
6   Who *was* Foucault and why does Hornby bring his name into his article?
7   What is the tone of the sentence *I'll bet you're fun at parties*? What does it show about Hornby's view of people who do *know who Foucault is*?
8   Explain the 'case' Hornby makes for the song 'I'm Like a Bird' in the third paragraph.

Language and vocabulary

1   Explain the following words as they are used in the text: *inane; encompass; forgo*.
2   Explain the following phrases: *narcotic need; dreamy languor; bruised optimism; anaemic and stunted peers*.
3   Hornby uses a variety of language from the sophisticated to the colloquial. Quote examples of both and explain how they are used for particular effect.
4   Explain the effect of using the words *anyway* (paragraph 2) and *See* (paragraph 3).

Sentence structure

Analyse the effect of:
◆   parenthetical brackets
◆   semi-colons and colon
◆   continuation dots
◆   dashes
◆   questions
◆   varying sentence lengths.

 ## TASK

Choose a subject about which people have strong and conflicting opinions. It could be footballers' fees; junk food; the legal age for driving; third world sweatshops – or anything else which interests you.

Write two provocative paragraphs on your chosen subject, addressed directly to those who hold the opposite view to yours.
◆   In the first paragraph, present your argument in a reasonable, persuasive way.
◆   In the second paragraph, change your tone. Challenge and provoke your audience directly.
Include:
◆   a variety of sentence structures and punctuation for deliberate effect
◆   direct questioning of your readers
◆   a variety of vocabulary, including the sophisticated and powerful
◆   contrasting persuasive and argumentative language.

People are passionate about many different things, from motor bikes to guinea-pigs. Reading has been Francis Spufford's passion since childhood. Text A is from his memoir, where he records his childhood absorption in reading.

Text B is an advertisement for a multi-activity trip from an adventure travel company, aimed at people with a passion for physical challenge.

Text A

The Habit

'I can always tell when you're reading somewhere in the house,' my mother used to say. 'There's a special silence, a *reading* silence.' I never heard it, this extra degree of hush that somehow travelled through walls and ceilings to announce that my seven-year-old self had become about as absent as a present person could be. The silence went both ways. As my concentration on the story in my hands took hold, all sounds faded away. My ears closed. Flat on my front with my chin on my hands or curled in a chair like a prawn, I'd be gone. I didn't hear doorbells ring, I didn't hear supper time called, I didn't notice footsteps approaching of the adult who'd come to retrieve me. They had to shout 'Francis!' near my head or, laughing, 'Chocolate!'

I laughed too. Reading catatonically wasn't something I chose to do, it just happened, and I was happy for it to be my funny characteristic in the family, a trademark oddity my parents were affectionate towards. Though I never framed the thought then, stopping my ears with fiction was non-negotiable. There were things to block out.

Text B

RUSH HOUR

a new and it seems, popular concept in 2002 ...why not seek out the top adventure spots of the world and partake of as many challenging activities as humanly possible in a week or less? Not for the faint-hearted, these trips are designed for those who get off on high adventure, full-on fun and excitement in the great outdoors. Whether in the air, on land or on the water, we provide all specialist kit and instruction but you mustn't forget your 'give it a go' attitude. Though we stay at some great places with food and drink to match, relaxation and sleep are optional, and timid couch potatoes need not apply.

gps navigation
arapaho
abseil
kayaking
ice climbing
tyrolean traverse
canoeing
paragliding
caving
mountain biking
bob sleigh
igloo build
rock climbing
cross country ski
skidoo
canyoning
hydrospeed
dog sled
via ferrata

Understanding and interpretation

Text A

1 Explain exactly the '*reading silence*' which Francis's mother can sense.
2 Explain how Francis reads 'catatonically'.
3 How does the suggestion in the final sentence, *There were things to block out,* help the reader to understand the 'catatonic' nature of Francis's reading?
4 How effective is the first sentence of the text?
5 Analyse the effectiveness of the simile *like a prawn*.
6 Explain the meaning and effectiveness of the metaphor *stopping my ears with fiction*.

Text B

1 Identify the specialist vogue words and expressions (colloquial words and expressions which are used *now*). Analyse how they give this text its particular tone.
2 Analyse how the sentence structure and language challenge the reader.
3 Which qualities are required in someone who will sign up for one of these trips?
4 The picture accompanying this item in the brochure shows a lone climber on a rock above a canyon. How effective is the title *rush hour*?

Making comparisons and cross references

1 Compare the audiences for which these two texts have been written.
2 Analyse the contrast between passivity and action in these two texts.
3 Compare the vocabulary and its effects in the two texts.

TASK

Writing for different audiences

1 Choose one of the activities from Text B. Write a paragraph for the brochure which will make the reader think 'Wow! I've got to go!'
   - Appeal to your reader's adventurous spirit.
   - Arrest your reader's attention in every sentence.
   - Use imperative verb forms.
   - Use colloquialisms for special effect.
   - Use verbless sentences for special effect.
   - Use vigorous language and expressions.

2 Write the opening paragraph for a speech on the motion 'The most absorbing hobby has got to be...' The choice of hobby is yours!
   - Address you audience effectively.
   - Arrest your audience's attention throughout.
   - Vary your sentence structure.
   - Use sophisticated vocabulary to impress.
   - Make at least one emphatic point.
   - Use at least one illustration or example effectively.